A Map of My Heart

HOW TO WRITE

Michelle Lovric

Designed by AB3 and Michelle Lovric
Copyright © 1995 Michelle Lovric,
Covent Garden, London
Produced by Imago
Printed and bound in China
Contributing Editor: Melissa Stein
Technical Editor: Brian Burns

First published in the United States of America and Canada by
Shooting Star Press Inc., ®
230 Fifth Avenue, Suite 1212
New York, NY 10001
Library of Congress Cataloging-in-Publication Data
ISBN: 0 - 1-57335-355-8

George Bernard Shaw

HOW
TO
WRITE
Love
Letters

Michelle Lovric

SHOOTING STAR PRESS

Prelude

I undertook my first American author tour when my book, *Love Letters* AN ANTHOLOGY OF PASSION, was published in February 1995.

I was a media virgin, and arrived in New York with some innocent expectations of the kind of questions interviewers and members of the public would ask me about this unusual book. In fear of drying up, I armed myself with fluent anecdotes about the exciting detective work of tracking down the original letters and the diplomatic coups of persuading people to let me photograph them, about the technical triumphs of recreating the original wax seals, about what it was like to work in the most famous Reading Room in the world – and similar scholarly questions.

Nonsense. In America, the touring author and the media enter into a simple and elegant alliance, whereby in return for the warm spotlight of attention upon his or her offering, the author delivers not worthy miniatures of the new work or even personal revelations, but entertainment and – just possibly – *information*. In every interview, in all media, at book signings, in Green Rooms, in taxis, as the book climbed into The New York Times best-seller list, the incandescent question, the inevitable question, often the *only* question I was asked was: *How do you write the perfect love letter?*

I learned to answer that question and this book is the result.

Michelle Lovric, Covent Garden, London, September 1995.

Contents

LOVE LETTERS – THE UNLOST ART

Nothing exists unless it is on paper.

Anaïs Nin

Let the heart speak! Permit Love to use the pen, and he will find his own words and forms.

How to Write – A Pocket Manual

Before words, there is, of course, desire. Language is the thread joining that desire to its object, explaining its needs, expressing its cries. In the absence of eyes to tell and feed upon, or kisses to calibrate, words are all we have to say: "I love you *this* much! How much do you love *me*?" Almost everyone, at some time in their life, will love someone else so much that they must write it down. And who could suppose that out of just 26 alphabetical letters, we could create and transmit such pleasure as we do in our written caresses?

However, it's rarely enough to write merely "I love you". These three words, in theory the most compelling of human exchanges, have been debased by familiarity. They mean everything or nothing, unless rescued by personal detail. It is the dilations and embellishments of "I love you" that beguile, the novelty that fascinates, the personality of the writer that seduces.

As writers of love letters, we are the source, the guarantor of sincerity, the editor and the stylist. The love letter is our heart on our sleeve, our battle standard, our essence, our indelible signature, our emotional fingerprint, our private well of memory, our own ghost of kisses past, our true secret self.

If we were given the whole correspondence of any person, be it Simone de Beauvoir or our own grandmother, we would first turn to the love letters, knowing that there we would find the most intimate, unconscious portrait of the correspondent, and we would see them at their most personal and their most appealing. Moreover, a love letter illuminates not just the person who wrote it, but also, by refraction, the person to whom it is written. Of all literature, love letters are the words most often kept, and most often burnt.

We write letters because *anyone* can send flowers.

We write letters because we want to be close to someone who is physically absent.

We write letters because we dare not speak our love in the presence of the loved one. Letters allow us the graceful expression of words we might be unable to stammer out because of nervousness. In a letter, we can deliver a thousand volts of passion, without faltering, and without danger.

We write letters because they are more potent than verbal declarations. A letter can be the best expression of our love and admiration because it is a considered thing, and time spent on a love letter allows refinement towards perfection.

We write letters because they allow the reader to have their own unwitnessed reaction, to think about what is offered, and to reply in their own time.

We write letters because they last, even when the love that inspired them has gone, leaving little other trace.

We also write letters because *someone wants them*.

This is partly because we are all insecure. We cannot hear often enough that we are loved, or tell the loved one about the delight we take in them. We can scarcely believe our luck.

But spoken words are slippery, evanescent.

The public will always give up its dinner to read love letters.

·5·

George Jean Nathan

Most anthologies about love endow it with an unalloyed deliciousness, supposedly sweeter than chocolate. But for practitioners in the late 20th century, love is less a delectable swoon of lyricism and more a neurotic emergency on all fronts – intellectual, cerebral, emotional and physical. Writing and receiving love letters are graceful palliatives for the lonely, the lustful, the needy and the disbelieving.

Catullus, the Roman poet, wrote in the 1st century BC: What a woman says to her desirous lover should be written on the wind and running water. In other words, it has no substance. However, what she *writes* can be treasured forever.

A love letter is a real affirmation. It cannot be imagined. It cannot be denied. It cannot be contradicted, unless perfidious. It's physically there, defying our insecurities and uncertainties.

Unlike a telephone call, a love letter can be brought out, thrillingly unfolded, time and time again, to reanimate sumptuous memories or to relive half-forgotten pleasures. Years later, a letter may even deepen in meaning as layers of subsequent events and feelings are superimposed. It's less effort to prattle amorously on the telephone – but there's a reason why these conversations are called 'sweet nothings'. Nothing is all that's left behind at the end, no matter how torrid or how tender the exchange.

In this respect, a love letter is the same as a love fax, which is the same as a printed-out love E-Mail – so long as the lover commits the sentiment and the embrace to words and onto paper, or even onto a screen. It's only a telephone call that leaves no trace, gives the lover nothing to put under the pillow or carry in the breast pocket.

Love likes to be tactile. A letter is literally a touch of our lover's hand. A posted love letter is, of course, charged with a more tangible sensuality, than a fax or E-Mail. The letter comes with the knowledge that the fingers of the beloved will brush the very same sheet of paper the writer has loaded with love.

·6·

I WOULD HAVE ANSWERED YOUR LETTER SOONER, BUT YOU DID NOT SEND ONE.

Goodman Ace

The mysterious processes of the post invest letters with an extra romance. We write them; we address them (enjoying the feathery caress of the pen on paper as we stroke out our lover's name); we seal them, we stamp them with a small painting, and drop them, irretrievably, into an inscrutable box, to be handled by strangers on their journey. Then there's the light-headed period of waiting until we might fairly think the letter has been received – and the fervid anticipation of the arrival of the reply. The postman becomes the mystic go-between, the lover's second-favorite person in the world.

It's sometimes said that the telephone, fax and E-Mail have killed the letter. That's a very narrow view. In fact, the unique new technology of the late 20th century has liberated the letter from mundane business, elevating it to a very special position. I found this to be very much the case in my research for manuscript letters to reproduce as facsimiles, where an important part of the criterion was that the letter must have good red meat all through. So often, a wondrous letter would trail off into domesticity, as with Dorothy Osborne asking William Temple to find her some French tweezers, or into professional or military detail, as with Napoleon breaking off the most lyrical love letter to Josephine to tell her how many Italians he'd slaughtered that morning. Nowadays, these items of information would be transmitted by the telephone or the fax, and the letter would be reserved for heartfelt matters.

Thus, the love letter has survived, and even profited from technology – and people are still writing love letters for the same reasons as they have done throughout time: because they can't help it, and because they want a response.

Being in love is an altered state – everything is heightened, including the creative urge. Many people have written of bursting with feelings that need to be expressed. Love always wants to proclaim itself, to write itself everywhere: in the sand, in the fire, with flowers, in the wind. When in love, many people resort to poetry, but far more write love letters. One is for public consumption: the other expresses private passion, and is therefore all the closer to the heart, being, as it is, more intimate, more truthful, more revealing, more specific and more moving.

The voice flies from the lips to mingle with the winds, to be lost without an echo... Written down, it may continue sounding on, as from a trumpet tongue, through all time ... W. C. Fowler

AS

LONG AS

THERE

ARE

POSTMEN,

LIFE

WILL

HAVE

ZEST

William James

In a love letter, we entertain, we inform, we gloat and we perform. We show our best possible selves being as loveable as possible. Love can transform accountants into poets. It can also turn perfectly sensible people into embarrassing drivellers, as passion, which would be better bridled, pours itself out in meaningless exaggeration.

Sometimes, people write because they are so obsessed with their lover that they cannot do anything else — as Balzac wrote to Evelina Hanska, in 1835:

> *I cannot bring together two ideas*
> *that you do not interpose yourself*
> *between them. I can no longer think*
> *of anything but you.*

Or Vita Sackville-West writing to Virginia Woolf, in 1927:

> *I am reduced to a thing that*
> *wants Virginia*

Often, people write to make a proposition of one kind or another. The love letter has been described as a form of direct-mail marketing, and this is not entirely mischievous. One of the most flagrant of these pitches is reputed to be from the rakish Prince de Joinville, to the

actress, Rachel Félix, on seeing her for the first time in the 1840s. He wrote simply:

> *Where? When? How Much?*

Her equally notorious reply was:

> *Your place. Tonight. Free.*

The absence of the loved one poses a special problem: after all, if they really loved you, how could they bear to be absent from you? The only solutions: catalogs of longing, reassertions of the bond between writer and reader, delicious and enticing projections.

Sometimes, like Olive Lewis, an English woman writing to her future husband during the Second World War, people write to relive their own ardent and romantic experiences, especially when they are separated:

> *Now in the quiet of the evening and*
> *in the warmth of the bed a drugged*
> *and dreamy feeling steals over me*
> *and I am with you once more.*
> *Lying here I love to think of you*
> *near me, your arms encompassing*
> *me, my head buried in your*
> *shoulder, catching the rhythm of your*
> *breathing and living for a few*
> *exquisite moments as one being — I*
> *said I was dreaming, darling, but*
> *I am so delightfully intoxicated,*
> *relishing such heavenly moments with*
> *you that I wish it to go on forever.*

Such letters are often concerned with the prologue (endlessly recounted) and the epilogue (sadly post-mortemed), but best of all, the future, glowingly delineated. Writing a passionate letter can arouse the writer as much as the recipient and describe what *will* happen in such a compelling way that it *does*.

People also write love letters because being in love is a state of generosity. One loves the whole world, and the lover in particular. One way of showing love is with a tangible tribute: three-dimensional love tokens, such as rings, flowers, photographs and locks of hair. But the love letter is more potent than all of these because it is entirely personal. Like a ribbon-bound curl or a portrait, it cannot come from or express anyone else, but added to its individuality is the fact that it is a fusion of mind and heart. A good love letter is also an intellectual exercise, informed with affection; a paper kiss in the form of an infallible dart, carefully directed at the emotional pulse of the loved one.

The thwarting of desire has inspired some of the best love poetry and love letters. The saddest love letters (alas very frequently occurring) are from imploring lovers, whose passion remains sternly unrequited. Writing can be the revolt against rejection, the refusal to be silenced, the defiant assertion of the position of lover and beloved; the refusal to accept an emotional assassination.

Sometimes, the object of love is not entirely or truly the point. Sometimes, the lover merely desires desire, and the loved one is no more than the tool of that desire. When such a love object is lost, then it's the loss of love that we weep for, not the loss of the beloved. Quite a few writers have shown themselves more fond of their literary passion than of the person who apparently kindled it.

De Musset, Byron and Pushkin come to mind.

There are a thousand reasons why *not* to write a love letter: you might look ridiculous; you may have misinterpreted the situation; you may give offence. Doubts like this can prevent you from writing a letter that could, in fact, cure pain, bring joy and reanimate lost hopes.

A book cannot teach you how to write a perfect love letter, any more than a book can teach you how to make love. Possessing a love that's worth expressing is the first prerequisite. But effort is also required: more effort than it takes to dial a number and murmur a few forgettable endearments.

A love letter should give pleasure in the writing, as well as in the receiving. This book is for people who find it difficult to write letters, and it's also for people who would like to be better at it.

It's for people who are in love (but who are tongue-tied in person), who may find, in the model letters following, a template for their thoughts that they can imprint with their own feelings. It's for people who would like to leave a lasting testament of their love, and would like that testament to be creative, touching and beautiful.

A SHORT HISTORY OF EPISTOLARY ROMANCE

Unlike war or empire, love leaves little trace on the landscape. The archaeology of love is a difficult business: only the *written* kisses survive the brief, incandescent alchemy of love. And yet, some of the world's best literature can be found in the letters of lovers who have successfully ignited each other's passions with their prose.

Where does the love letter fit into literature? In some ways, all public literature is merely a long letter to an unknown reader, whom we hope is out there for us, listening, understanding, appreciating. Writing feeds our obsession with self-expression. Private literature, or letters, are something else again: real thoughts from real people to others they truly love, or wish to.

Fictional love letters have been the backbone of many novels. The epistolary – or letter novel – was staple fare in the drawing rooms of the 18th and 19th centuries, starting with Samuel Richardson's *Pamela*.

Famous Epistolary Lovers

The media of the lover's message has evolved from etched stone tablets, through bark, parchment, quill pens and paper to typewriters, faxes and E-Mail. However, the message itself has changed remarkably little. There was a time when everyone knew how to write a graceful letter in a legible hand. This art has been lost, though the love letter as an art has not been lost: it has simply become more precious.

For anyone interested in the subject of love letters, there's an inexhaustible well-spring of passion to be found in the primary sources. Below is a very brief historical sketch of some published bodies of romantic correspondence, which are both inspirational and beautiful.

The Bible's astonishingly voluptuous *Song of Solomon* may be the earliest example of a kind of love letter.

Letter writing was esteemed by the Romans as a liberal and polite accomplishment. Cicero and Pliny wrote homely, affectionate and even passionate letters to their wives.

From early times, the Japanese have written 'morning after' letters. The lover would send an elegant note to his mistress of the night before, praising her skills, and send with it a flower or branch. The foliage would indicate the state of his desire for her: waxing, waning, delicate or strong. In *The Pillow Book of Sei Shonagon*, a 10th-century courtesan describes the process in enjoyably matter-of-fact detail.

One of the earliest and best known of Western epistolary romances was that between the ill-fated French lovers Heloise and Peter Abelard, who fell in love around 1117 when she was a brilliant student aged 17, and he her 38-year-old tutor. But her outraged uncle Fulbert had Abelard castrated and Heloise confined in a convent for the rest of her frustrated life. The tragic lovers were permitted to correspond. Heloise's letters are explicit in their sensual longing; Abelard's, not surprisingly, under the circumstances, are more philosophical.

As a literary form, the love letter probably started in the early Renaissance. The Age of Chivalry produced a series of amatory correspondences that were based on extravagant but chaste compliments and excessive self-deprecation. All physical passion was sublimated, and unconsummated adultery became the fashion. Absence of corporeal pleasure did not much disturb Dante Alighieri in his adoration of the untouchable Beatrice. Her early death in the 1290s made no difference to the miracle that was his love for her, written not exactly in letters but in *The Divine Comedy*, his poetic tribute. Courtly love is further exemplified in the graceful and utterly discreet sequence of letters between the much-maligned Lucrezia Borgia and the poet Pietro Bembo in 16th-century Italy.

The somewhat earthier letters of Henry VIII of England to Anne Boleyn implore her, with a degree of veiled threat, to become his mistress; he then encourages her tenderly. One letter also exists from Henry to Anne's successor, Jane Seymour. Chillingly, one sees similar endearments and his same need to point out, constantly, that he is paradoxically the servant and the sovereign of his lover, with power of life or death over her. His daughter, Elizabeth I, also received her share of love letters.

Meanwhile, in France, Henri of Navarre was writing delightfully informal love letters to a series of mistresses, of whom the most famous was Gabrielle D'Estrees. From the same period, Walter Raleigh's last letters to his wife are very moving, in a stately way.

Dorothy Osborne and William Temple courted intelligently, playfully and passionately by mail throughout seven years of political difficulties that kept them apart. They finally married in 1654. Thomas Otway, the English poet and playwright, wrote hopelessly to the actress Elizabeth Barry, in the last quarter of the century. Starved of love, Otway eventually decided to starve himself to death, and succeeded. Heloise's spiritual sister was the famous languishing lover of the late 17th century – the sad Portuguese Nun, Marianna Alcoforado, seduced and abandoned by Noël Bouton de Chamilly, a French knight. Her letters to him (only occasionally suspected of being unauthentic), are amongst the most searing in any literature, ancient or modern. In France, the lady of letters, Ninon de L'Enclos produced a series of deathless epistles on love and how to survive it.

> *A letter has been a problem for lovers ever since - well, I suppose that it has puzzled the suitor of all ages and of all nations. I can fancy the youth of ancient Rome standing before the scribe ... just as well as I can fancy the youth of Young America with lifted pen thinking how he shall address his beloved.*
>
> Ingoldsby North

·11·

By the 18th century, love letters were becoming more visceral and more personal. In France, Julie de L'Espinasse tore her heart out and presented it to the disinterested Comte de Guibert. Indeed, tormented French epistolary romances of the 17th and 18th centuries deserve not a paragraph but a chapter of their own.

Notable epistolary scoundrels at either ends of the 18th century were Jonathan Swift and Robert Burns, both adept at running several relationships simultaneously. Their duplicity is immortalized in their love letters. Swift seduced both the gentle and loyal Esther Johnson (whom he called "Stella") and the spirited Esther Vanhomrigh ("Vanessa") in a most cowardly and cold-hearted way.

Robert Burns was equally incapable of fidelity. He first fell in love with Ellison Begbie, a servant-girl, and propositioned, wheedled and eventually proposed to her, but his most serious written romance was with Agnes McLehose. They christened themselves "Clarinda" and "Sylvander", and exchanged many ardent letters, despite the fact that Burns was settled with a common-law wife.

At the other end of the fidelity spectrum was the delightful Richard Steele, the essayist and politician, who wooed and won his beloved Mary Scurlock (whom he called "Prue"), during the first decade of the 18th century. His courting letters are charming, but it is the letters written after their marriage that reveal him as the most affectionate and faithful of husbands. He was not ashamed of showing raw tenderness in his letters, nor of apologizing. Also surprisingly modern, though this time in their angst, are the letters of Lady Mary Pierrepont when conspiring, amid much explicit soul-searching, to elope with Edward Wortley Montagu.

George Farquhar, a brilliant writer of comedy, wrote movingly to his leading lady Mrs Oldfield, during the same period. Taking everything just a little step further was Laurence Sterne, author of *Sentimental Journey* and *Tristram Shandy*, who spent most of his life deliriously in love with someone or other. His most passionate letters were written, during his later years, to the hard-nosed Elizabeth Draper (his "Bramine"). These letters are flavored with a delicious humor.

Samuel Johnson pursued a long, intellectual love affair with the clever and charming Hester Thrale. Johnson's biographer, James Boswell, undertook what he hoped would be a sex tour of the continent and broke a few hearts with his dilatory love letters, though not as many as he would have liked.

There emerged at this time a game of amorous wordplay in which the participators, such as the notoriously fashionable Beau Brummell, amused themselves by making smooth verbal or written love without actually engaging their deeper feelings. Courting couples from this period include Lord Peterborough and the Countess of Suffolk, whose letters are full of witticisms and epigrammatic definitions of love, but almost empty of real emotion. Alexander Pope's mincing epistolary minuets with the Misses Blount also fall into this category, as do the gallant letters of Horace Walpole to the Misses Berry.

But there was a distinct change in the tone of love letters with the progress of the 18th century. The Romantic spirit swept away the earlier devotion to empty frivolity and artificial ritual in love-letter writing. The French had already led the way, with the new intellectuals blowing cobwebs out of stylized love: Voltaire, Rousseau and Diderot applied their penetrating arguments to the state of the boudoir as well as to the library. The great German writers, Goethe and Schiller, wrote frank and engaging love letters, and considered this personal literature not trivial but vital to the pursuit of happiness and self-knowledge.

There's a definite sense of authenticity in Napoleon's welter of obsessive letters to Josephine in the 1790s. The Comte de Mirabeau, languishing in a dungeon on his father's instructions, spent his time writing impassioned soliloquies addressed to Sophia Ruffey, with whom he had earlier eloped. On the other side of the channel, Lord Nelson and Lady Hamilton conducted their affair in unlaced language. A whole culture of love letters grew up around the legendary, ethereal Madame Récamier, who successively frustrated Lucien Bonaparte, Chateaubriand and Benjamin Constant, a lover she shared with

her friend, the literary lioness, Madame de Staël.

Mary Wollstonecraft's letters to her American lover, Gilbert Imlay, show a sobering sense of reality. Imlay abandoned her and their infant daughter. This correspondence is all the more pathetic for the intelligence that informs her suffering. Wollstonecraft eventually married a London publisher and writer, William Godwin, to whom she also wrote some notable love letters. She died giving birth to their daughter, Mary, who was later to marry the poet Percy Bysshe Shelley and become famous as the author of *Frankenstein*.

Thus, a new generation of lovers was born: The Shelleys were friends of the melodramatic George Gordon, Lord Byron. Indeed, Mary's kinswoman, Claire Claremont, bore a child by him. Byron was the object of much epistolary pleading – not just from Claire, but from a crowd of clamoring women, including the notorious Lady Caroline Lamb, who is thought to have forged some letters from him in return. Byron, meanwhile, wrote love letters to Annabella Millbanke, whom he unhappily married, and immoderately, to his half-sister, Aurora Leigh. The subsequent scandal saw him exiled to Italy, where he became entangled with the young Countess Teresa Guiccioli, to whom he wrote the last love letters of his life. Literary Italian lovers of the same period include the novelist, Ugo Foscolo, whose letters, addressed to innumerable different women, are blistered with tears and racked with extravagant sighs.

Tangential to the incestuous Byronic circle was the frailer, feverish John Keats, whose unhinged but lyrical letters to Fanny Brawne are often cited as the most beautiful ever written. Less dramatic, but equally sincere and interesting, are the love letters of William and Mary Wordsworth, and Jane and Thomas Carlyle.

As the 19th century drew in, Honoré de Balzac devastated forests in his voluminous pursuit of Countess Evelina Hanska. Victor Hugo wooed Adèle Foucher and was himself romanced by Juliette Drouet in a ravishing correspondence that continued for 50 years. Briefer and crueller was the relationship between Gustave Flaubert and Louise Colet, in the middle of the century, in which Colet flayed herself against his cerebral brick wall. More mutual were the overcooked histrionics of George Sand and Alfred de Musset, and the fervent celebrations of Franz Liszt and Marie d'Agoult. Later, Sarah Bernhardt spawned her own private industry of love letters.

In Germany, the writers von Kleist and Hölderlin were respectively dying and going mad for love. The great German composers found both amatory and musical uses for their quill pens. Mozart surprises with his rowdy endearments to his wife, Constanze. Beethoven dashed off one of the world's most famous letters to his unknown (but much theorized) "Immortal Beloved", while Robert Schumann and Clara Wieck smoothed their prickly path to matrimony with a blissful correspondence. Later in the century, Richard Wagner pursued love in his letters to his wives, Minna and Cosima, and the actress Judith Gautier. Gustave Mahler, too, had love letters as well as symphonies to express.

In America, husband-and-wife lovers with style and imagination included: Nathaniel and Sophia Hawthorne, Samuel Clemens (Mark Twain) and his beloved Livy, and Woodrow Wilson and his adored Ellen. In Russia, Catherine the Great showed a lusty approach to sexual politics, and later, Alexander Pushkin pursued his wife (and other people's wives) with both ardor and humor. Tsarina Alexandra deluged Tsar Nicholas with cosy, domestic love letters.

Back in England, the highly literary romance of the poets Elizabeth Barrett and Robert Browning culminated in their elopement in 1846. John Ruskin wrote trembling missives to his fiancée, Effie Gray. Charlotte Brontë pursued Professor Constantin Heger, in an affecting but hopeless campaign of letters. At the turn of the 19th century, George Bernard Shaw and Ellen Terry luxuriated in letters of rapture, uncluttered by

actual physical contact. Shaw again exploded into lyricism with his later passion for the actress Beatrice Campbell, whom he nicknamed "Stella".

The 20th century has brought explicit sexuality to the art of love letters. Some of the most scalding are by the French poet, Paul Eluard, to his ex-wife Gala (who married Salvador Dali), and the self-consciously erotic pyrotechnics of Anaïs Nin and Henry Miller.

The last 100 years have also brought us: Franz Kafka's neurotic epistolary wooing of Felice Bauer and Milená Jesenská; the tender, sometimes childlike epistles of Katherine Mansfield and John Middleton Murry; Edith Wharton's sadly insightful letters to W. Morton Fullerton; Eugene O'Neill's and Sherwood Anderson's numerous letters to their many wives; W.B. Yeats' written rhapsodies to Maude Gonne; D.H. Lawrence's early romance with Louise Burrows; James Joyce's gentle but raw letters to Nora Barnacle; the playful passion of Duff Cooper and Lady Diana Manners; Zelda Sayre's vehement letters to F. Scott Fitzgerald before and after they married; the legendary metaphysical and simply physical love of Simone de Beauvoir and Jean-Paul Sartre; Frieda Kahlo's dramatic relationship with Diego Rivera; Winston and Clementine Churchill's happy union; Dylan Thomas's lyrical letters to his temperamental wife, Caitlin; and many more.

War has always been good for the mass production of love letters. Two World Wars created loneliness and anxiety on a vast scale, reflected in a rash of urgent love letters. Danger loosened tongues and inhibitions: no one wanted to die without having made love. Ordinary people became poets of love and death. Romances that might have taken a lifetime to unfold were crammed into leave days. In the carnage of war, first declarations were tragically turned into last mementos. The war museums of the world, and the attics of the present generations, are full of the correspondence of lovers and spouses separated, by war, sometimes for years, sometimes forever.

The present century has allowed us to to write and read homosexual loves openly for the first time, and suddenly another great body of beautiful, passionate literature has come to light: Oscar Wilde's rose-strewn letters to Lord Alfred Douglas; the highly articulate romance of Vita Sackville-West and Virginia Woolf; the solicitous partnership of Benjamin Britten and Peter Piers were just the start.

Perhaps the true extent of the love-letter writing of this century will not be understood until the next, when those ribboned packets, maturing in those many attics are rediscovered and rejoiced in by the curious and appreciative children, grandchildren and biographers of today's lovers.

·15·

THE FATE OF LOVE LETTERS

When researching *Love Letters* AN ANTHOLOGY OF PASSION, I was able to contact some living writers and ask permission to use their letters. Nearly everyone was delighted, as it was felt that the publication of the letter was yet another tribute, this time in public, to the loved one.

People who have been concerned with a breach of their privacy – or considerate about the privacy of others – have destroyed their own letters, sent and received. Charles Dickens refused to have some of his letters published. Catherine Pozzi burned hers. Samuel Johnson was more philosophical: when asked if he would be mortified at the thought of his letters being published posthumously, he replied, "when I am dead, you may do as you will".

More morally ambiguous is the business of selling original love letters. Oscar Wilde wrote a wry poem about the auctioning of Keats' love letters. Edith Wharton asked for her love letters back when her affair with W. Morton Fullerton became one-sided. Instead, he later sold them. George Bernard Shaw once withheld permission when Beatrice Campbell asked to print his love letters, saying: "No, I refuse to play horse to your Lady Godiva."

Love letters have sometimes been edited by the recipients, who feared that the intimacy expressed might blot the subsequent reputation of both partners. Years after their marriage, Sophie Hawthorne scribbled through and actually cut out passionate passages in letters from her husband Nathaniel. She worried that posterity would judge him to have overleapt the bounds of decency then laid down for a fiancé.

Some people wrote their love letters with a definite eye on publication. George Sand, for example, used her correspondence as raw material for a thinly disguised novel about her stormy romance with Alfred de Musset. He did likewise, and both agreed to have their love letters published while they were still alive.

A Legal Note

The author is the owner of the copyright of the letter. This right may only be waived by written permission. The actual physical letter may be sold, but this does not give the owner of the letter the right to reproduce the letter. The author can veto publication on grounds of infringing copyright and of breach of confidence.

The duration of the copyright is for a period of 70 years in the USA and 50 years in Europe and Australasia from the author's death. There are numerous technical exceptions to all the general principles. It is no doubt best to abide by an emotional principle: would the publication of this letter hurt anyone?

THE PUBLICATION OF LETTERS ADDS A NEW TERROR TO DEATH ...
Dr Arbuthnot

·16·

PRACTICAL ADVICE

There's little point in writing a love letter unless you do it well.

Most people who fall in love find it all too easy to write (it can be more difficult to stop!). In a matured romance, familiarity and shared concerns ensure plenty of material to exchange. Most advice is probably needed by a first-time love-letter writer, or by lovers who want to use letters to progress, enhance or save their love affair.

The most important piece of advice about any love letter? Just make sure you write it! Not only on Valentine's Day, or when you have a particular reason, but any time.

Presentation: Write a Well-Dressed Love Letter

You should dress your first love letter as carefully as *you* would dress for your first date. Sins against aesthetics may not be a problem in your particular relationship but, on the other hand, you want to reflect an appealing image of yourself in everything you send to your loved one. Seize every opportunity to show what a desirable lover you are, or would be.

·17·

Your Own Hand

Write by hand, unless there's a good reason not to. At the very least, sign in your own handwriting. Don't put a love letter through the office franking machine, or write it on your business letterhead, unless the letterhead is part of your 'story'. Give it a sense of occasion. Make it special.

Your signature is a symbol of who you are. Make it memorable, so that it tugs the heart every time your lover sees it, just as if you had stroked their eyelids with a feather pen.

Another reason for promoting the 'hand-made' feeling is that, at this early stage, people need reassurance that what they are receiving is genuine and not a direct-mail pitch to any number of suitable candidates (as has famously been done on the Internet).

Know that your penmanship will say things about you. In your own handwriting there are nuances and possibilities that a typed version can never convey. For example, Isadora Duncan once explained to Gordon Craig how her love for him flowed like the waves of the sea – she intensified her words by the charming device of drawing waves all around a line of the word "LOVE" repeated and repeated. Dylan Thomas's tiny beetle tracks expressed his isolation and fear as much as his words.

Write me, write me, write me! ... Your letters are the world's prettiest blondes.

Victor Hugo to Louise Colet

'It was very pleasant to me to get a letter from you the other day. Perhaps I should have found it pleasanter if I had been able to decipher it. I don't think that I mastered anything beyond the date (which I knew) and the signature (which I guessed at).

There's a singular and perpetual charm in a letter of yours; it never grows old, it never loses it's novelty ... other letters are read and thrown away and forgotten, but yours are kept forever – unread.

Thomas Bailey Aldrich

But a handwritten letter has a stronger emotional impact only if it's legible. If your handwriting is truly appalling, it's an act of courtesy to type. However, as a typed letter is always slightly more remote than a handwritten one, always acknowledge the distance created and try to bridge it with the charm of your apology.

Private communion with your personal computer is intellectually very little different from time spent with a quill pen and paper. You're still alone with thoughts of your loved one, turning your feelings into sentences, committing your caresses to words.

Some simple visual adjustments can make your letter easier to read and understand. Remember to leave a generous margin – at least an inch all around the edge of the paper, and to create paragraphs, especially if the letter is longer than one page.

One final note of warning about typed letters or E-Mail: you may type accurately, run it through the spell-check and print it out on pink paper, but it still won't necessarily make sense or sing lyrically. It's all the more important to infuse a typed document with the romance that drains out of it.

Paper

Your choice of paper tells tales on you, too. On a practical level it may help you to avoid being obvious about certain delicate matters. For example, you don't need to say, "Here is my phone number – I hope you will use it", if the number is discreetly printed or written on your letterhead. Similarly, make sure you supply the address for a return letter.

Paper to reach for: a thick, luxurious texture will add a sensual element to your letter. It's also harder to throw away a thing of beauty and obvious value, especially if it's the work of a loving hand.

There's something elegant and lasting about black ink on cream or white paper. Anything else is a statement of something else.

Scented, pastel note paper is not necessarily the love-letter writer's prescription pad. You can express an astonishing variety of things by your choice of paper. You could use paper that shows you already have something in common. For example, you can say: "I'm writing on green paper because it's obviously your favorite color, and it's also mine – I've noticed you often wear it and you look wonderful in it." Or, if you already know that your lover likes a particular Victorian poet, you could write your letter on the back of some suitable verses. Again, this will emphasize the empathy between you, the sharing on a deep level, the subcutaneous attraction.

A tentative or nervous love letter might be written in pencil on semi-transparent paper, to give the appropriate message. Recycled paper may impress your correspondent with your ecological concerns, or could simply look somewhat dirty. Always consider what your recipient wants from you.

Until early this century, most letters were written bifolium: a single sheet of paper folded in half, to make four pages, like a brochure. You could re-invent this style for a love letter, and even fasten it with a wax seal.

Paper to avoid: anything decorated to the point where it's hard to read text over it; notepaper that is in itself a visual cliché, for example, sprigged with roses, or spotted with hearts. Keep away from lined paper – the epistolary equivalent of a bunch of tired flowers from the nearest gas station. If you want to add visual interest, decorate your letter with stamped motifs. Charming old woodcuts and engravings have been revived and are available commercially. You can create your own personal letterhead for your relationship.

E-Mail and fax lovers have fewer opportunities for three-dimensional pleasure than devotees of 'snail mail' (conventional post). If using a fax, remember that the transmission may render tiny details illegible. There's another drawback: fax paper fades, taking its words with it. So if you receive or send love letters by fax, always make sure that a plain paper copy is made, or you have come no further than the telephone. Finally, the public nature of office fax machines can add an agreeable frisson to transmitted love letters, but always be discreet and considerate.

Pens

A fountain pen is inevitably more pleasurable to use and its work is more pleasing to the eye than a ballpoint. You will yourself enjoy the sensual experience of writing the letter if you work with smooth flowing ink, and if you're physically enjoying the writing, then the likelihood is that you'll produce a physically enjoyable letter.

If you really want a response, try sending a lovely pen to your lover, with a sheet of paper and a stamped envelope addressed to you. Only the dullest of lovers would not take the hint.

How to Write – A Pocket Manual

USE BLACK INK – THE BEST AND BLACKEST OF BLACK INK.

·19·

Multimedia

An 'activity letter' can be amusing for both parties. A chunky envelope stimulates desire and curiosity. Delay can increase gratification, as your lover tears open a heap of tiny, individually wrapped mementos, all the time reflecting on the imagination that you showed in creating this pleasant torture. Make the enclosures worth the struggle.

Remember also, that a tangible object is a kind of corroborating physical evidence of your love, just like the letter. It says: This is a real thing. So is my love. It's also a way to say: I've touched this and now it's touching you.

But physical tributes can be clichés too. Avoid the single, pressed rose or the cute soft toy. Try appealing to all five senses, for example: a monogrammed handkerchief soaked with your special fragrance; a tape of your own voice reading a love poem; a silk scarf; a single heart-shaped chocolate. Or you can send a silent love letter by cramming a handful of petals into your lover's wallet, secretly.

Clever ways to deliver your love letter

- Written on a leaf, or pinned to a tree in your lover's garden.
- Left in lipstick or soap on the bathroom mirror.
- Written in indelible ink – in a tiny envelope – planted inside an ice-cube in a drink.
- Rolled up in a series of tiny notes and tucked into closed-up tulips. As the flowers open, in the warmth of a room, the notes will appear.
- Pinned to a tempting food in the fridge.
- Re-label a wine bottle with a love letter.
- Inscribe your message on a fan.

Another winsome idea is to make your own collage celebrating your relationship. For example, as a unique souvenir of a blissful day together, you could assemble a ferry ticket, a blade of grass from the field where you lay together, a snippet of poetry you quoted that day, a photo you might have taken. Arranged artistically, a collage can be a startlingly effective tug on the emotions.

Or draw a map of your heart, showing the part your lover occupies, or a map of your life, with all paths leading to your lover.

Another clever idea, if you're separated for a number of weeks, is to make a personal advent calendar, with a new little window to be opened every day, each one revealing a tender, personal message or an apt quotation from a love poem.

I Love you

BE MINE

You could also adopt the ancient Japanese idea of sending a flower with your letter to express an extra nuance of feeling. For example, a sequence of letters could be accompanied by a sequence of rose-leaf, rosebud and maturing rose, as passion mounts.

There's something to be said for varying the media of assault – a fax one day, a letter the next. A telegram (described by Eugene O'Neill as "the lazy man's love letter"), may galvanize a positive shock. A series of quick-fire faxes, spinning a story, can be fun.

Locating a Comfort Zone

Composing a love letter should confer as much pleasure as reading one. You should make the writing of it an island of peace and happiness; do not come to the love letter in a bad mood, or too busy to write properly. The old letter-writing manuals (see p.31) agreed on this, and often gave explicit instructions. In *The Art of Writing*, from the early 1700s, John Newbery recommends that the chair should be high enough to sit easily and your desk or table at the height of your middle. The book or paper should be at your left side ... "Thus seated ... you may write with all the Freedom and Ease imaginable: No Nervous Flutterings, no Numbness, or Stifness ..." You may find it inspiring to go to a place that has meant something to you as a couple, or to sit in a park where you have walked together: green shades *do* have a habit of generating green thoughts.

Preparations in Advance

A piece of good advice from Lewis Carroll (Charles Dodgson, mathematician and author of *Alice in Wonderland* as well as hundreds of whimsical and affectionate letters to young girls): start with addressing and stamping the envelope:

"What! Before writing the Letter?" Most certainly. And I'll tell you what will happen if you don't. You will go on writing till the last moment, and just in the middle of the last sentence, you will become aware that 'time's up!' Then comes the hurried wind-up – the wildly-scrawled signature – the hastily-fastened envelope, which comes open in the post – the address, a mere hieroglyphic – the horrible discovery that you've forgotten to replenish your Stamp-Case – the frantic appeal, to every one in the house, to lend you

a Stamp – the headlong rush to the Post Office, arriving, hot and gasping, just after the box has closed – and finally, a week afterwards, the return of the Letter, from the Dead-Letter Office, marked "address illegible"!

This may sound fatuous, but do make sure you spell your lover's name correctly. It's worth a little covert research in the case of a first letter. Nothing is more distancing than being addressed as "dear Sarah", when you're really Sara.

When addressing the envelope, it never hurts to write "Personal and Confidential". These words always inspire a little shiver of anticipation. Don't decorate the outside of the envelope with kisses and cute little sayings. Your reader may not want fellow householders or colleagues to know about their romantic life, especially before they know about it themselves. (An envelope embellished in a subtle or original way is a different matter altogether.)

At the top of the letter, it's a nice touch to write, as was common in the 17th and 18th centuries: "To Erik", "To Nancy", "To my Husband", or whatever is appropriate. And you should always date your letter. It may be, or become, part of a sequence, and someone may someday want to recall this romance and trace its history.

Salutations and Valedictions

The form of address, or salutation, is vital. If it's a first letter, then use "Dear..." It's risky to start a first love letter with "My beloved Dan," unless you're already sure that such a proprietorial salutation is welcome. Allow intimacy to unfold gradually. If you're fortunate enough to develop a romantic correspondence, then "Dear" may melt into "Dearest" and gradually "Dearest Love" and perhaps "My only Love" and beyond. Seize every opportunity to show each nuance of increased tenderness, as soon as you dare.

The form of signing off can be developed along similar lines. The first letter may well end with "Yours sincerely" but might more creatively end with "Yours, in breathless anticipation of your response". In turn, this can lead to "Yours, in joy and wonder".

If in doubt about the appropriate degree of affection, refer to the last letter you received from your lover. Look at the last words, and if they are

Ah, young man and young woman! You write a "love-letter." Do you know that you are forming a bond which shall be to you for good and evil, just as far as you are honest and true, now and forever, to that bond?

Ingoldsby North

warm, travel further towards the fire. If they have written "with love" you could write "with tender love" or "with all my love". The only proviso is that these two statements must be true.

A postscript (a P.S.) is acceptable, but it must be a fresh little entity of its own, and not a sloppy way of refining a thought clumsily expressed earlier. A postscript can also be used to throw into the shade any little matter that you do not wish to inflate into a big issue.

Logic and Sequence: How to Draft a Love Letter

A love letter is a very important document. It can change the way someone feels about you forever. When you decide to write a love letter, you're not merely making a gesture, you're taking a significant step,

Therefore, it's vital to know yourself before you try to write to someone else. Know what you want to give and know what you want to ask of the person to whom you're writing. If your thoughts ramble uncertainly, then your written words will certainly follow the same inconclusive and bewildering path. At the very least, this is not endearing. Clear thoughts must then be expressed in a logical *sequence*, or your message will still be unclear.

Before you write the letter you should ask yourself the following questions:

- To whom are you writing this letter? (You must take into account what you know about the person – things they might like to hear and the points of reference you share.)

- Why are you writing this letter? (What do you want to achieve? Is it a first romantic approach, or is it to celebrate an evening of bliss?)

Thinking about these two things should help you plan what you're going to write and how you're going to write it

It may be a good idea to establish a set of key points in organized sequence. You can trail off into the rosebushes with your language later, provided that the logical framework is there.

A man is known almost as well by the words he uses as by the company he keeps. Choose both from among the best.

How to Write – A Pocket Manual

·23·

Your key points, for a first love letter, might be something like this:

- You may be surprised to receive this letter, but ...
- Something happened to me when I met you. It was like ...
- You're wonderful in ... ways.
- I would like to see you again.
- I suggest ... place and ... time, because ...

Having written these skeleton notes, wrap your letter in compelling ideas and vivid images, making sure that before you begin to write down each sentence, you have it complete in your head.

If you find it hard to start, remind yourself that a love letter should be like a conversation between lovers. Think of what you would like to say if the person you love were with you at that moment.

Don't repeat yourself. If your reader does not understand the first time, they can re-read the letter. Unlike in conversation, you can make your point without interruption.

If it's to be a truly earth-moving letter, then you should also write a full draft – a tradition from the days before carbon paper or word processors, which also enabled the sender to keep a copy of his prose. You should also keep a copy of any love letter you send. It may well be the most important thing you ever write. Also, if it's misunderstood, you have a chance to revisit it, in order to explain yourself more clearly.

Be careful. No letter can be guaranteed to be private, even in the short term. Letters are permanent and, if you make an injudicious or slanderous remark, it may have results that are more than painful. Remember also that there are legal limits about pictorial and written material that may be sent by mail.

If you're responding to a powerful letter, build on what is positive in it, and subtly undermine the negative. For example, if your lover is critical, ignore it, but if there is praise, however scant, show gratitude and then respond with even more generous compliments.

Finally, do not make any promises you cannot or do not intend to keep.

Having written your draft, try, if you can, to read it through your reader's eyes – and ask:

- Does the letter say exactly what you mean?
- Will the recipient see anything in it which you do not intend – anything more, anything less?

- Have you included something you might regret after mailing it?
- Are you going to enclose anything with it – a flower, a poem or a gift? If you have mentioned such a thing, put it in the envelope immediately. Otherwise, you're likely to find it lying on your desk after the letter has been mailed.

The drafting process enables you to exorcize unworthy feelings. For example, if you're angry with your lover, your first draft may reveal that rage as petulance and jealousy. A love letter gives you the opportunity to present yourself in a more dignified role. Unlike in a lover's tiff, you can edit out things that you know you'll regret later.

If your letter is likely to cause pain or anger, do everyone a favour: don't mail it immediately. Put it aside until the next day. Re-read and then send it, if you must. Putting your violent emotions on paper may have been cathartic enough. When you re-read your letter, imagine how you would feel if it were directed at you. As Lewis Carroll says: "This will often lead to your writing it all over again, taking out a lot of the vinegar and pepper, and putting in honey instead ..."

Also use the review stage to eliminate inaccuracies. A careless letter not only reflects badly on you, but is discourteous to the person you love.

History is full of lovers writing letters that request their own destruction. They seldom are destroyed. Perhaps the best principle is never to write a letter that needs to be destroyed. (And remember that a love letter *not* sent can also detonate.)

Ask for the Moon, but not the Stars

Don't ask for too much, especially in a first love letter: perhaps another meeting, or a drink. To commit your life to someone in the first letter is to invite worry that you're deranged. Perhaps you are. But be quiet about it for now. If you're attracted and just want an opportunity to get to know the other person a little better, then say exactly that.

On the other hand, if it's nothing more subtle than lust you're feeling, you could also be specific. There's no point in wasting time, if you don't want a long-term relationship. It depends entirely on what you want to achieve. Don't ask for anything you can't handle. Beware of getting what you want.

On this same theme: keep it short. If you don't know the person well, then you could be spinning fantasies that are potentially boring, alienating or disturbing to the recipient.

An American saying

In letters I desire clarity and brevity, penetration and grace, wit and gravity.
Marsilio Ficino

A love letter sometimes costs more than a three-cent stamp.

As you *may* be wasting your time, don't waste more than you need, unless you're collecting material for a novel. Don't try to write the letter to end all letters. Remember, love letters usually come in series, so keep something back for next time.

Be Specific

Be very specific about what attracts and delights you. Sometimes this will unlock your thoughts and help you get started. If it's her way of bursting into laughter at the exact same moment you do, or the way he brushes his hair back from his face just before he makes his point – describe it. People can never hear enough about themselves, in sufficient detail, ever! But be careful of objectifying your lover with long lists of conventional descriptions. Your reader will respond only to the intimate details you have lovingly observed.

Think about – write about – the intangible attractions too: the intelligence or perceptiveness of your reader. Take some time to understand your own passion. Then the telling of it will make the beloved feel good about himself or herself. If the aspects you describe are the things your lover would like to have recognized, then the hoped-for empathy between the two of you becomes more real.

If you're writing an erotic letter, be specific about your own unique gifts (and don't be modest). Make your lover see, through your eyes, how utterly desirable they are. There's no more effective form of seduction. Be as demure or provocative as you wish, but if, for example, you aim to arouse (and are sure you won't offend), be as graphic as you can. What *kind* of caresses – lingering or feathery, moist or hot? *How long*? How many times? *That* position? *What* color? Remember that writing is also a good way to rehearse for the ultimate performance. Be truthful about your own fantasies: it's the only alternative to telepathy if you want your lover to help you enact them.

Do not Pursue the Trivial

Keep boring domestic and professional details out of a love letter. Some of the great love letters of history have been spoilt by jarring domestic or professional details. Make this a letter that the recipient will want to keep forever, a monument to love and passion, undiluted by trivia, fussiness and boring technicalities.

Make a word picture ... putting into it the squirrel as

If you're nervous about subject matter to pursue, these basic strong ingredients cannot be out of place in a love letter:

- That you're missing them and you're not doing well without them. Tell them (briefly and entertainingly) what you're doing in their absence, and what you would do if they were present, highlighting the present longing in comparison with the hoped-for future pleasures.
- Ask your lover how *they* feel: are *they* spellbound by the same magic? What are *their* symptoms?
- What a relief it is to be able to spill out your pent-up feelings in this way.
- How much you loved their last letter.

Responsiveness

You should make it plain if you're replying, initiating a correspondence, or following up a letter you've already sent. Always thank someone who has written to you: this graceful act should be rewarded, every time. Doing so also helps to allay common fears about letters not arriving.

If you're replying to a letter, it should be in front of you. Answer all the questions and points it raises. Otherwise, you run the risk of your correspondent thinking that you did not understand or read their letter properly. But never give a merely efficient, mechanical reply to a letter. Add to it. Take the writer's thoughts and run with them. If they write to you using a metaphor, develop that metaphor creatively.

Before replying, make sure you know what the currency is. When your correspondent says "love", is this word expressed in the emotional equivalent of pesos or dollars?

Writing Style

Letter writing is talking on paper. But in ordinary conversation, we repeat ourselves, speak ungrammatically, express ourselves inelegantly. Such faults pass by unnoticed in speech, or may at least be excused and forgotten. But written

well as the mountain - little things as well as great.

down, mistakes are a permanent witness to ignorance or carelessness. You should think of your love letters as a record that may be preserved by your lover long after the relationship, or even your life, is over. Commit nothing to paper that will throw a shade on your memory.

This book is not the place to propound a complete English usage. In a love letter, an error of grammar is not a punishable offence. A split infinitive, can more easily be forgiven than an insincere statement or a cliché.

Individuality is the greatest charm of a letter. The most cherished letters are those in which the writer's soul has been poured out on paper. So, write a letter *that no one else could write*. You want the person you love to be attracted to the real you, so don't project a fantasy about who you are. Don't shelter behind your pen or your typewriter, pretending to be bolder, more aggressive, more honest, more eloquent, more, or less, in love than you really are.

The best love letters approach a conversational style: a good letter should exclude anything that sounds forced or pretentious. To test this, read your draft aloud. If it sounds unnatural, even in your own speaking voice, then it will read unnaturally at the other end.

A love letter should not be a soliloquy, even if you don't know the recipient well enough to be intimate. Use the word "you" as often as possible, especially in sentences containing the word "I". It's the verbal equivalent of touching someone. It will make them feel closer to you.

Avoid copious underlinings and capitals: they soon pall. There's rarely a justification for triple exclamation marks (!!!). Limit yourself to one exclamation mark only in a letter and make sure you are saying something worth exclaiming about. Don't write all in capital letters. IT LOOKS LIKE SHOUTING!

Banish clichés from your love letters. Apart from being boring, they sound insincere and will make it sound as if writing love letters is a routine thing for you. Falling in love is *not* routine. It should ring a thousand original creative bells in your head.

Being in love may make you feel like a teenager or a small child, but always avoid wince-inducing diminutives such as "Doll" or "Babykins" unless they're already part of the accepted vocabulary of your romance. They may sound cute to you, but they can actually diminish the person you're describing. Your lover will be more beguiled by seeing him or herself refracted, like a kaleidescope, in your eyes: a complex jewel, ever changing, ever more dazzling.

Avoid meaningless exaggerations, such as "you're the most beautiful girl in the world", unless you qualify or decorate them with some kind of original thought. For example, Dylan Thomas used this exact phrase, but added "... and it's worth dying to have kissed you", thereby transforming the tired phrase into something dramatic and lyrical.

Another kind of cliché is to describe the conventional erogenous zones with conventional rapture. Try to be more original. Certainly, you may linger over the eyes, but you could show more creativity by describing the erotic impact of the tendril of hair escaping from behind their ear.

If you can't find the exact word you want, consult a Thesaurus. Use surprising language where you can. It refreshes all parts of the brain, both yours and your lover's. For example, instead of saying: "I love kissing you and looking at you", you could, to paraphrase Swinburne, say "all your face is honey to my tongue and all your body pasture to my eyes". You can freshen a sentence quickly by substituting strong and vivid verbs for the weak and overused ones. Instead of merely "loving" your reader, why not cherish, hold dear, adore, desire, idolize, embrace, fondle, caress, dote on, delight in, lose your heart to, or be smitten, beguiled, enchanted, captivated, titillated by them?

Be original, but not merely for the sake of being clever. Long words can sound pretentious. If you have the urge to use a special or esoteric word, it might be a good idea to check it in the dictionary, even if you think you know what it means. The dictionary definition (which may well be the one consulted by your puzzled reader), may carry different nuances to those you intend to convey.

Jargon is generally unsuitable in a love letter. A love letter is not the place in which to show off your technical expertise. The exception would be if you share a profession with your lover and you want to set up a witty or extended metaphor. Similarly, foreign phrases should be used only only when you know or can safely presume that your reader is familiar with the language.

Avoid padding, such as "at the end of the day" and "the rest is history". Such phrases have been so abused as to have no meaning. Finally, avoid ambiguous words unless you mean to be ambiguous.

Never mind the length. Long letters have gone out of fashion, along with kept women and lives of leisure. It's no longer an occupation to write letters: it's a luxury.

A Compleat Introduction to the Art of Writing Letters

To express far fetched Conceptions, requires a Stiff and formal Language, which is not more unpleasing to the Ear than disgustful to the Heart; that which is most Easy is most Natural, and Nature never fails to please.

·29

Sometimes, letters must be long, but in terms of effectiveness, a letter that has good meat all through, however short, is better, and more effective than nine pages of sloppiness, diluted with gossip and detail. Never confuse length with quality.

It is, of course, harder to be brief and concise than it is to ramble on, but it can also be more tantalizing to write something short, leaving the reader craving for more. For example, love letters can be written as postcards. One powerful sentence accompanied by an image can be amazingly effective. A series of postcards can be exciting — you're simultaneously communicating with words and pictures, intensifying what you're sharing, progressing the relationship on several levels, sometimes with humor.

Wit

By all means, be funny. But be very careful of teasing and irony. When you're not there to soften a sarcastic comment with a smile, then it could be felt very sharply. So, if you're making a joke, let it be right over the top, so there's no mistaking it for a barb. Lovers are notoriously thin-skinned. Similarly, it's hard to convey the nuance of a raised eyebrow to someone you don't know very well, especially in writing.

Humor in a love letter can come from a genuine wit, or just from clever handling of language. Letters, being short, must depend on one-liners. Puns are a natural, if the object of your desire has that kind of sense of humor. Try for a sting in the tail. Leave them laughing, thinking how witty you are and how good it would be to spend time in your company.

Another amusing tactic can be to write to your lover under a ridiculous assumed name or title, knowing that this ruse will be detected. As a 'Family Planning Officer' you can insert *double entendres* you might otherwise not dare.

A love letter should be a treasury of bright and happy thoughts; not a cauldron of seething despair. Try not to complain too much. The piteous lover deserves nothing but pity, as Richard Steele once observed.

Worst of all is sending a perfectly correct love letter that sounds like a business letter — too polite to charm, too perfect to be human.

I have made this a rather long letter because I haven't had time to make it shorter.

Blaise Pascal

LOVE-LETTER-WRITING MANUALS

This book follows a centuries-old tradition. The offering of love-letter-writing manuals dates back to the early 1600s. The books described below are just a tiny selection from a large library of charming volumes. Most books include a miscellany of advice on the whole field of correspondence, grammar, law and poetry.

They often list correct forms of address for titled or professional people and give rules on spelling. This reference section is always followed by a selection of model letters to imitate, often amusingly grandiose in style, but many manuals also include letters from sailors, soldiers, butchers and their sweethearts, in earthy dialect, but all aspiring towards a nobility of spirit. Cheerful plagiarism was very much the fashion in the early manuals. Letters from famous people, unattributed, were included along with models penned by the author or editor.

The old manuals have titles such as *THE ACADEMY OF COMPLEMENTS* Or, a New Way of Wooing (1685) and *THE Young Secretary's Guide* (1687) in which the prefatory Epistle to the Reader hopes that he will "gather from the sundry choice Flowers scattered in this Garden of profitable Recreation, some Honey of Improvement ..." A very early volume was Angel Day's *The English Secretorie*, of Methode of writing Epistles and Letters, which dates back to 1607. This boasts a chapter on "Epistles Amatory" among many others, such as "Expostulatorie" (angry) and "Laudatory" (praising).

In *Wit's Improvement Or, A New Academy of Complements* (1715), there's a somewhat laborious secret sign language for clandestine lovers, and a diagnosis of the spiritual meaning of moles. It suggests effective opening gambits to be used when "accosting gentlewomen", both verbally and in writing. Model letters are given for various situations. It concludes triumphantly with a series of love poems and finally some healthy country dancing.

Also dating from the early 1700s is *The Amorous Gallant's Tongue Tipp'd with GOLDEN EXPRESSIONS OR, THE Art of Courtship refined*. This delightful little book includes various choice raptures for recycling and also some short letters to copy – for example: "Your Beauty is the Pole-Star of my Soul, and brings my wandering Heart toss'd on the Billows of Inconstancy, to the desired Haven of its Rest.";

·31·

THE
COMPLETE ART
OF WRITING
LOVE LETTERS;
OR, THE
Lover's Best Instructor.
IN WHICH
The TENDER PASSIONS are displayed in all Forms, real or feigned; as discovered in the

SINCERE			INSIDIOUS
MODEST			BASE
HONOURABLE	} LOVER {		PERFIDIOUS
RAPTUROUS			TREACHEROUS
PASSIONATE			DISSEMBLING
FORLORN			MERCENARY

With Rules and Instructions to the FAIR SEX, how to make a happy Choice of a GOOD HUSBAND. Exhibiting in a series of Letters, a variety of Truth and Falshood, Sincerity and Treachery, Happiness and Misery, with several Examples in both Kinds. To which are added, some elegant Forms of
MESSAGES for CARDS.

Heaven first taught Letters for some Wretch's Aid, Some banish'd Lover, or some captive Maid; They live, they speak, they breathe what Love inspires, Warm from the Soul, and faithful to it's Fires.
POPE.

and the Amorous Gallant also busies himself with interpretations of "all Sorts of Dreams, with many other Things, both pleasant and profitable to both Sexes".

A partly satirical volume from 1736 is *POST-OFFICE Intelligence OR, Universal Gallantry, BEING A COLLECTION OF LOVE-LETTERS ... returned into the General-Post-Office in Lombard-Street, the Parties to whom they were directed being either Dead, or removed from their usual Places of Abode*. Its introduction, attributed to "the most judicious and celebrated Dr. Donne, Dean of St. Paul's", addresses the metaphysical joys of correspondence:"Writing of Letters, when it's with any Seriousness, is a kind of Extasy, and a Departure and Secession and Suspension of the Soul, which doth then communicate it Self to two Bodies." Dr Donne is further supposed to be of the opinion that "if any Carrier of London, going to Oxford or Cambridge, should chance to be robbed of his Letters by the Way; a Man would, peradventure, meet with more Wit, in that poor Budget, than in Some whole Book of Foreign Modern Printed Letters, of Some other Nations".

From the same period, *LETTERS Written TO and FOR PARTICULAR FRIENDS*, is most concerned with sincerity, attempting to expose the "empty Flourishes, and the incoherent Rhapsodies, by which shallow Heads, and designing Hearts, endeavour to exalt their Mistresses into Goddesses, in hopes of having it in their Power to sink them into the Characters of the most Credulous and Foolish of their Sex. Orphans, and Ladies of independent Fortunes, he has particularly endeavour'd to guard against the insidious Arts of their flattering and selfish Dependents, and the clandestine Addresses of Fortune-Hunters, those Beasts of Prey, as they may well be called, who spread their Snares for the innocent and thoughtless Heart."

In 1795, approximately, there appeared: *THE COMPLETE ART OF OF WRITING LOVE LETTERS OR, THE Lover's Best Instructor*. It's introduction is is worth quoting as a typically florid period piece: "Selfish or sinister views are too apt to gain ascendancy in the scale of love; and the word sincerity is too frequently made a trap to ensnare the unguarded virtue and simple innocence; honour is abused to the worst purposes; and the solemnity of oaths and vows, which outh to make an Atheist tremble, prostituted to the service of Hell and the Devil."

The Victorian period saw the tradition continue, but in less emotional style. The niceties of etiquette and society manners became far more important. The Victorian manual are far less red-blooded, and much less entertaining, with notable exceptions, such as Ingoldsby North's *BOOK OF LOVE LETTERS*, published in New York in 1867. The author pays a great deal of attention to the fact that letters are the key to establishing compatibility before marriage and, as such, must air all vital subjects, including aspirations, not forgetting pecuniary matters, in order to ensure a successful union. In a lecture entitled "The Utmost Candor", North points out: "I need not inform the intelligent reader that bad habits, for instance, are necessarily, especially in American society, secret habits ... But a man who is addicted to wrong courses and hides his propensity is vile beyond description. Fortunately none such will buy this book."

THE MODEL LETTERS

♥ OVERTURES AND SOLOS ♥

·33·

The model letters in this book are a skeleton guide - source material, food for thought, an attempt to provide some freedom from anxieties about form and style. They should be used and adapted for your own specific situation: No book has ever been, or can be, written that can provide love letters simply to be copied and sent. The whole point of a love letter is its individuality. Your love letter is you at your very best.

AUTHOR'S NOTE: IN THE MODEL LETTERS, I HAVE, IN SOME CASES, INTERCHANGED THE SEXES AT RANDOM. THERE IS NO INTENTION TO APPLY SEXUAL TYPECASTING TO THE DIFFERENT KINDS OF EPISTOLARY EXCHANGES. THE SEX OF THE WRITER MAKES NO DIFFERENCE. THERE ARE NO MALE OR FEMALE LOVE LETTERS; ONLY GOOD OR BAD LOVE LETTERS.

OPENING ONE-LINERS

Wouldn't it be nice to get to know each other while we both have teeth and hair?

LOST: ONE HEART, SCARCELY USED BY ONE CARELESS OWNER. LAST SEEN THROBBING IN YOUR DIRECTION

·34·

Would it be too dangerous for us to meet again?

Other people have chemistry, but with you it felt more like Nuclear Fission...

Where? **WHEN?** *Forever?*

(Reply)
Your place. **TONIGHT.** *Depending...*

DID YOU **ORDER** ME? I FEEL AS IF I WAS **MADE FOR YOU,** SPECIALLY

*W*hy did you let your eyes rest on me *like that,* and smile at me with *that* smile, and speak to me in *that* voice? Now nothing can ever be the same again.

JUST AN HOUR WITH YOU HAS PUT MY BRAIN BACK IN TOUCH WITH MY HEART

I'M THE ONE

The Long-Lost Lover
a reverie

I was a boy. At an age well before any awareness of the passions and dreams of a man, and yet I would dream of a woman. A particular woman. She was mine. She was not maternal, nor a sister nor a friend, but I loved her. I did not understand the love. I did not seek it. But it was strong. It distracted me when I was awake, and the discomfort it gave me sometimes caused me to wish it away. It has never left me.

She had a pale face set against soft dark hair. Her voice sparkled like water, and echoed in my mind long after she spoke. In her presence I felt the warmth of her love. Only once have I seen hands as delicate as hers.

Although I try not to, I know I still seek her.

When we first meet we will hardly touch. That will be later,
*   very much later.*
We have plenty of time and will wait for the moment.
I will hold your hand and feel the warmth of your
*   presence.*
That is all I crave, for the moment.

To me you are a woman in a painting/ photograph by a friend. I visited her often, and she would speak of you. She would explain you to me — the way that close friends do when giving their descriptions of those they love. My fascination with you, in that picture, has not left me.

I remember well my feelings when I knew that I would meet you. I knew that I would blush and betray my dreams.

We met. A brief exchange was all there was between us. You sat on the floor by the fire. I sat on a chair in the corner opposite you.

I had a clear view of you. I tried not to stare. I was dazzled by you. You were beautiful.

But I cannot remember you.
I can only remember the picture.
When will I see you again?

The New-Found Lover

an opening gambit

Can you imagine if I'd decided not to go to the party on Friday night! I'd never have met you and everything would be different. All night from the moment we were introduced, I saw only your face, heard only your voice, wanted only to be with you. If you had stayed five minutes longer, I'd have been forced to kiss you.

Something about you – I'm not sure what it is – makes me want to know you better. Although we barely spoke, we were friends instantly. And there's something else there: something that makes my imagination *rage* with the idea that we could be far more to each other.

It was wonderful to watch you, scintillating in the crowd, but I am afraid it wasn't enough. I want you to myself, just for an evening. I want to see you sparkle *just for me*.

But I don't want to scare you off by asking too much at this stage. I would just like to see you again, for a few hours, just to talk, just to listen.

If you think I'm being too bold, or too rash, you have only yourself to blame. You're just too perfect, too exactly perfect, for me to walk past and ignore the possibilities you've opened up for me.

I'm enclosing a copy of a poem by Rainer Maria Rilke for you. It's about what I am afraid will happen if you do not say "Yes". Say "Yes"!

·36·

You who never arrived
in my arms, Beloved, who were lost
from the start,
I don't even know what songs
would please you. I have given up trying
to recognize you in the surging wave of the next
moment. All the immense
images in me – the far-off, deeply-felt landscape,
cities, towers, and bridges, and unsuspected
turns in the path,
and those powerful lands that were once
pulsing with the life of the gods –
all rise within me to mean
you, who forever elude me.

You, Beloved, who are all
the gardens I have ever gazed at,
longing. An open window
in a country house – and you almost
stepped out, pensive, to meet me. Streets that I chanced upon, –
you had just walked down them and vanished.
And sometimes, in a shop, the mirrors
were still dizzy with your presence, and startled, gave back
my too-sudden image. Who knows?
Perhaps the same
bird echoed through both of us
yesterday, separate, in the evening ...

Rainer Maria Rilke

The Amenable Lover

a reply to the opening gambit

Yes! That same bird echoed through me, yesterday, in the evening. And I'm so relieved that you wrote to me, because if you hadn't, then I would have had to write to *you*.

Ask me to do whatever you want. I don't think there is anything I would refuse you. (Actually, I can't stop thinking of things I wish you *would* ask.)

Your letter was so lyrical – I think I want to sing it! I can hardly believe that I've inspired such eloquence in you. I've already heard about your work, and about how many people love and admire you, so I can't think what made you pick *me* out of the crowd at the party – except that you felt what I felt – a shock of recognition, like a wrong number at midnight, an empathy, a lightning attraction that's still illuminating everything. Suddenly, I seem to be looking at everything through your eyes. How could that happen, when I've only known you for such a short time?

I'd be enchanted to meet you again. Let's make it soon. I'm not a great believer in delayed gratification. Let's meet in a garden – one you've gazed at, longingly.

Yours, still dizzy from *your* presence ...

37

SHORT VERSION

I adore the way you spell my name. I adore receiving your poems like caresses and your words like kisses. I'd adore seeing you again ...

LIGHTNING INJURY:

LIGHTNING MAY PRODUCE SIMILAR INJURIES TO THOSE OF A HIGH-VOLTAGE ELECTRIC CURRENT.

INSTANTANEOUS DEATH MAY OCCUR.

ON BEING STRUCK BY LIGHTNING, THE CASUALTY IS STUNNED AND FALLS UNCONSCIOUS TO THE GROUND.

THERE MAY BE PATCHES OF SCORCHING ON THE SKIN, BURNS BEING DEEPER WHERE A METALLIC OBJECT, SUCH AS A WATCH, HAS BEEN CARRIED CLOSE TO THE SKIN.

CLOTHING MAY BE SET ON FIRE.

TREATMENT:
IF NECESSARY GIVE ARTIFICIAL RESPIRATION; TREAT BURNS.

The Authorized Manual of St John Ambulance Association and Brigade, 1973.

The Lightning Lover
love at first sight

*Y*ou might think it is extraordinary to receive a letter from someone you've never even met. But please keep reading. Even if you decide to refuse my request.

I've only ever glimpsed you once through the window of the place where you work, but I feel that, were we to meet properly, you'd be very important to me. You are already – more than I can say. I picture your face everywhere – imprinted on the snow, on rainy streets, suspended in leaves on trees. I always thought that "love at first sight" was a cliché or a lie. Now I know I was wrong. I think I am in love with you. It happened the first moment I saw you.

I don't know any mutual friends or colleagues who could introduce us. I did not want to alarm you by approaching you in person. Also, I can't trust myself not to say the wrong thing.

So this letter seems the right thing to do – to be courteous, to make sure that you don't think that I'm crazy. I am not – except in that other sense that exists only in song lyrics: I'm crazy about you.

Please give me a chance to meet you properly. Can I suggest the coffee shop next door to your workplace, on Saturday in your lunchtime? I won't keep you long. You'll recognize me: I'll be the one whose face lights up as soon as you walk in.

I hope that I haven't offended or frightened you. That's the last thing I want. And if you have no desire to meet me, then you can depend upon it that I won't intrude any further into your life.

There's no need even to reply to this letter. Just come, if you feel you can. If not, I'll understand completely. I won't be any less interested, so if at any time later you would like to contact me, my address is here – and I am here for you.

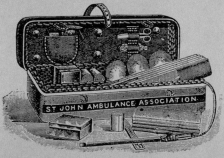

Tho' Cupid has often times assayed to wound my Heart, yet I have still despis'd the foolish Boy, and turned his Arrows back again unwounded. But at the Sight of your bright Eyes, my Heart was quickly pierced and I straightways became your Captive. For who cou'd hope to encounter with So many Charms as you are armed withal, and yet come off unvanquish'd?

The Amorous Gallant's Tongue

The Slow, Methodical Lover
a blueprint

When we first meet ...
We will part with a gentle kiss.

When we next meet I will be bolder.
You will tell me we said "go slowly".

At a cafe, by the river, I will touch your hair.
We will talk and with laughter learn more of each other.
We will part with a tender kiss.

The third time we meet we will have a whole evening, which
we know will turn into a night.
Remember we said that we would "go slowly".

We will talk for hours. You will tease. I will banter.
As we walk through the streets with you holding my arm.
You will seek reassurance that I will not hurt you.
I will ask you to trust me.

You will rest in my arms, as we lie on your sofa, with your soft
spellbinding music to keep us from moving.

That night, in your bed, I will softly caress you. The heat and
the passion is to be later.
Remember we said that we would "go slowly".
We will part with a loving kiss.

Yes,
yours,
my love,
·39·
is the right
human
face

Edwin Muir

The Poetic Lover

an intimation

Forgive me for not writing to you before.
It's just that when I met you, a kind of silence fell on me
— the silence that comes one minute before the curtain goes up.
The silence between the lightning and the thunder.
Are you feeling something similar?

The Prosaic Lover

an ultimatum

We have to come to some understanding. Do you want to see me or not? I absolutely cannot tolerate you stringing me along, treating me as someone to whom you send a letter or a fax every two weeks, allowing actual visitation rights a few times a year. I'm getting tired of this nonsense. I'm getting close to leaving you to your own devices. Let me meet you at your office at 5 p.m. on Friday — or not at all and never again. It's up to you.

·40·

The Mass-Mail Lover

Remember me?
I'm the girl you smiled at from the window of the train
on platform three on Saturday morning at 9.03.
I remember the moment precisely,
because time stopped for me just then.
I know that our smiles cut right through both of us.
I know you were about to leap out of the train and into my arms.
But just then the doors closed and the train carried you away
into the depths of the earth.
So I've had this photo taken of me,
standing in that same place where our eyes met,
wearing the same clothes,
smiling that same smile (though it's hard, without you).
I'm going to pin this photo up at every stop on your line.
If you find me, please ring me.
I want to take up where we left off.

...the Perfume of your Sweet Breath informs me, that your Mother fed on Roses, when she bred you.

The Amorous Gallant's Tongue

The Transforming Lover
an invitation beyond friendship

Can you feel this extraordinary thing happening between us? Can you feel friendship deliquescing into love? Can you feel my strength dissolving into tenderness? You are becoming part of me.

I find you in every poem I read and I hear you in every love song on the radio. My heart turns to honey when I think of you. You deserve sonnets, sonatas, sky-writing ... but this letter is the best I can do, the only way I can capture what I feel. (I hope you can decipher my hieroglyphics. I want you to know that this is the first letter I *haven't* written on the computer for five years – but I couldn't even think of using a machine to express my feelings for you.)

I've been struggling for ... with my love for you. Every time I see you, I am tongue-tied. The rapture foams silently in my heart and head, but the words just won't flow out of my mouth. The ironic thing is that this ridiculous inability to tell you of my passion is both my crime and its own punishment. Unless I tell you, I shall probably never know if you feel the same way.

Until now I couldn't get past my fear of rejection, my doubts that you could ever return my feelings. But it's come to the point where it's more painful to keep this love a secret than to risk exposing it to you.

I wonder how you will feel when you see the signature at the end of this letter?

41

The Curious Lover

Are you a great journey or a little walk? Are you the one? Or just one of them? I want to get to know you better. I want it to take a long time. I want to be like C.K. Williams (poem enclosed). I think I might – quite possibly – love you.

Here I am, walking along your eyelid again
toward your tear duct. Here are your
*   eyelashes*
like elephant grass and one tear
blocking the way like a boulder.

It probably takes me a long time
to figure it out, chatting with neighbors,
trying penicillin, steam baths, meditation
on the Shekinah and sonnet cycles

·42·

and then six more months blasting
with my jackhammer before I get in there
and can wander through your face, meeting
*   you*
on the sly, kissing you from this side.

I am your own personal verb now. Here I
come,
"dancing," "loving," "making cookies."
I find a telescope
and an old astronomer

to study my own face with,
and then, well, I am dreaming behind your
*   cheekbone*
about Bolivia and tangerines and the country
and here I come again, along your eyelid,
walking.

The Secret Lover

the solution to a romantic mystery
(This letter requires certain preparations in advance.)

It's now been more than a year since I first saw you, and knew from that moment that my life was in your hands. I never heard or saw your name without a shiver – half of delight, half of terror. I was the one who sent the roses. I was the one who rang you and played Mozart down the telephone line. I was the one who sent you the handmade Valentine card.

If you have any curiosity to find out who I am, I'll be at ... café tomorrow at 4p.m. I shall be sitting in the seat in the window, reading Diane Ackerman's book *The Natural History of Love*. (Have you read it?) I am tall, with long dark hair, and grey eyes. You've seen me before, though you may not remember.

You'll probably think that this letter is outrageous, that my imagination is out of control, that this proposition is preposterous, that this style of courtship is straight out of the 18th century. But at least come and see me. Give this mystery a chance to become a revelation. Something tells me you won't be disappointed.

Your no-longer-to-be-secret admirer ...

The Sunday Lover

a prayer for Indulgence

I came, I saw and I was conquered. No one ever had more to say to someone, and no one has ever been less able to say it. I went to church, where other people go to save their souls, and I, instead, lost mine to you. You were singing. I was speechless. You knelt, rose, sat, smiled, as if everything were natural. Meanwhile, I was in torment, in ecstasy, *in love*.

While I watched you, I forgot all the first Ten Commandments, but I formed an Eleventh in my head: That you and I shall love each other, only each other, always. While the choir was singing "Jerusalem", I was hearing in my head those beautiful words from the "Song of Solomon": "Behold thou art fair, my Love, behold thou art fair ... Thou hast ravished my Heart ... Set me as Seal upon thy Heart and as a Seal upon thy Arm, for Love is as strong as Death ..."

My thoughts during the service were wholly taken up with you. I've already installed you in your own personal shrine in my heart, where I worship you by the hour – for these sweet sins, I shall require both your mercy and the forgiveness of Heaven.

It's true that we've never spoken to each other, but I've heard the sweetness of your voice singing hymns and seen the gentleness of expression on your face when you pray – I feel that I have somehow been given a glimpse of your soul. So please accept this letter as the most reverent means I could devise to make your acquaintance. (Inspired by a letter from George Farquhar.)

The Monday Lover

Couldn't sleep, thinking about you. Woke up, thinking about you. Brushed my teeth, thinking about you. Washed my hair, thinking about you. Made myself smell nice, thinking about you. Listened to the radio, thinking about you. Went into dark tunnels, thinking about you. Rode the rushing train, thinking about you. Pretended to work, thinking about you. Walked home through dead leaves in the rain, thinking about you. Drank red wine, thinking about you. Sat by the fire, stroking the cat, watching the embers glowing, reading love poems, thinking about you. Went to bed, thinking about you. Couldn't sleep, thinking about you. Woke up, thinking about you.

Do you have visions, you sweet saint?

Byron Caldwell Smith to Kate Stephens

The Appreciative Lover
a review of a first date

I'm writing this at work. Actually, I'm in the middle of a production meeting, but I can't concentrate because thoughts of you and our evening keep pushing the facts and figures straight out of my head. How can they expect me to talk about budgets when all I can think about is the exact green of your eyes when the sun catches them?

I'm thinking about you in *your* production meeting today, and wondering if the same bright light is in your eyes as you frown over *your* budgets. I can picture you so clearly. I wish I could summon you in the flesh as quickly and easily as I can in my imagination. How can all these people talk about money? The only thing really worth anything right now is an hour with you.

I loved spending time with you. I'm so grateful to you for taking a chance, and agreeing to go out with me out when you barely even knew me. I hope that it was worth it for you, too.

For my part, last night confirmed everything I so wistfully imagined about you. I never experienced anything as delicious as that all too-short taste of your company. I remember exactly how I felt when you brushed your hair off your forehead, and the sunset lit up your skin all golden. But the strangest thing is what happened when I heard you speak to me: your voice was like the tone of my heart's own echo.

But tell me, what have you been doing since we saw each other? It has already been a day since we were together. It's hard to believe I must survive another six of them before I can see you again. Make it easier for me: write! even if it is just a line, a post-it, a postcard, an E-Mail, to tell me what you are doing and what you are thinking. Are you thinking of me at all?

I must stop now. It's a long time since my mind was attending this meeting, and someone is going to realize it soon. I can already see X looking at me in that way of his: I am sure he can guess what's going on. But I'm not ready to share you – or "us" – with anyone else, yet...

SHORT VERSIONS

Score after five hours together: seduction: partial; enjoyment: total; encore: please!

Mmmmmmm! Again?

The Reciprocating Lover

Thank you, thank you! Your letter made me blush, smile, laugh out loud. I can't remember the last time I felt that way. I am drunk with your words, just as I was intoxicated with your presence last week. You've filled up all my senses, beautifully, harmoniously and richly. I hardly know what to compare you to: You are the second movement of the second Brandenburg concerto. You are a jar of marmalade in the sun. You smile like welcome rain. You laugh like a diamond.

Really, I had no reasonable hopes of a letter from you so soon after we were together. But this morning, something made me linger in bed, dress slowly (having changed entirely three times – after all, what if I bumped into you in the street? I must look my best!). I swam through a delicious haze of memory and anticipation, each thought leading back to you. Suddenly it was 9.15 and I was late for work: late enough to be at home for once when the mail arrived. I must have known.

·45·

First, I enjoyed the strange, warm feeling of seeing my name in your handwriting, then I ripped your letter open and read it at once (twice). Then I read it three more times on the bus. When I got to work, I read it one more time before I started dealing with my in-tray, and during my coffee break, there it was again (twice) and I took it with me to the cafeteria at lunchtime. Everyone must have wondered about the secretive smile on my face. Now there's a coffee stain that makes the ink run in the first paragraph, but it doesn't matter. I know the letter by heart, anyway. Send me a new one as soon as you can. Every word will be cherished just as tenderly.

Gracious object of my pleasing thoughtes, and mistresse of all my inwarde happines, sweete were the lines you wrote, God wot unto mee ...

Angel Day

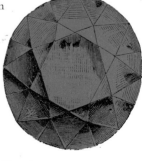

DUETS
AND DOUBLE
CONCERTOS

Come!
Come!!
Come!!!

Sarah Bernhardt
to Charles Haas

The Urgent Lover
a seizure

You've kidnapped my heart. While you hold it hostage, I can't concentrate for thinking about you. Someone asks me, "Would you like sugar in your coffee?" I think: She's sweeter than anyone I ever met. Someone says, "Can you do a meeting on Thursday morning?" My first thought is: I shall not see her till Wednesday night. You see, I *have* to see you before then, as all the time in between is totally wasted.

Do you really believe that I am capable of patience, self-sacrifice and restraint? No – Never! I can't see you without being swept away. I can't leave you without pain. This very moment I'm aching for you. I want you *now*.

I don't think you want me to suffer for you, do you? You don't want me glancing up at you shyly, or being tedious about coming to the point, do you? Everything about us has always been urgent. I don't want a slow burn. I want a sudden collision and a massive explosion. We must live to the full, or not at all. My desire for you bites like serpents in the night. It is not enough to squeeze my heart's blood into ink drops and and send it to you by snail mail.

This is what I can tell you. But there are more important things to *show* you. So, I want to see you tomorrow. I want to spend the whole day with you, and then the night. I have things to say with my lips that can't be written down.

Answer me by fax right now, or otherwise I shall imagine the postman struck by lighting, the mail train derailed and the sorting office burnt down!

And the only kind of fax I want to receive from you is the kind which should not have written. This is no time to be discreet.

(Inspired by letters from Richard Steele and Thomas Otway.)

SHORT VERSION
*My dear,
My darling,
do you love me?
Do you? Do you?
Do you,
sweetheart?
Say, do you?
Do you love me?
do you?
Say, you do.
Don't you?
Do you, angel?
Honey, Do you?
Do-you-Love-me?
Yes, my love,
I know you do;
but I want to
see you say so.
In writing.
Now!*

The Lunching Lover
a fax invitation

*L*ook out of the window. You'll see a taxi. It's for you. Get in and it will bring you to me. The menu is already on the back seat. Choose what you want to eat on the way. I don't want to waste a minute when we are together.

The Number-Crunching Lover

invitations to a second kiss

(I). I have deposited one kiss in our new joint account. I feel that this small opening balance must be augmented as a matter of urgency, and I hope that it can accrue interest as well as capital in the near future. Thursday?

(II). I was always good at algebra. I have this equation in my head: if X were me and Y were you, and the square of the hypotenuse was equal to the sum of the square on both sides, then our second kiss should be even better than the first one.

The Lamenting Lover
an E-Mail alternative

I am desolate. Our first kiss — our first exchange of software — our first interface — is over. It's gone. We can never have it again. Are you also suffering? Can we comfort each other?

I don't care if our second byte is simple or multi-tasked, mainframe or local area network, on your screen or on your spreadsheet — just so long as it happens. I'd like to share your database, search your memory, pull down your menus, key in some commands and download these feelings I have for you, even if they corrupt your hard disc. Something's going on deep in my circuitry, and I need to get on-line with it.

You are the Apple Mac of my eye!

The Morning-After Lover

Certificate 49·

This is to certify that yesterday, at ....time, on ....date, in ....year, at ....place, I,...................., was made the happiest woman in the world, in your arms.

Bathe your wanton Lips in sweet Dalliances

Wit's Improvement Or, A New Academy of Complements

The Lascivious Lover
a titillating invitation

I'm torn between the desire to see you, talk to you, show you things, read to you – and the feeling that the only way I can really say hello to you properly is to make love to you.

You have been in my head since we were together last week, and I am afraid that you are also finding your way into my heart. Several other organs are also reporting worrying signs. I need your elbows on my table, your hair on my pillow, your kisses on my lips, your hands on my body, your breath on my skin.

My blood lopes in my veins when I think of you, and my tongue flutters in my mouth. Lust ripens in my loins. Very specific fantasies unfold in my head. I picture you slippery with scented oil, all the better to be stroked. You look beautiful by candlelight, but it's in the dark that I see you best.

I'd like to write an erotic poem about you, describing all those parts of your body that fit so well with the corresponding parts of mine. It would be full of words like "addiction", "craving", "flesh" and "ecstasy". I want to pleasure you with words the way you pleasure me with pleasure. I want to describe the feeling I get just before, and the look you have just after, and how I forget everything in the world during – but what if someone were to find this letter?

SHORT VERSIONS

(I). What *is* it that's so seductive about you? I love your mild naughtiness. I love your skittishness. Most of all I love the glimpse of your (body part) when you wear (item of clothing). Its all too rare but I'll remember it forever, and the memory is music to my hormones. So, if you'll meet me tonight, and if you're *very* good, I shall allow you to use me physically. No part of me shall be forbidden to you.

(II). There's something wrong with me – I just can't get aroused physically. But if you really can't take "No" for an answer, well, you're welcome to come round and try.

Licence my roaving hands, and let them go,
Before, behind, between, above, below.
O my America! my new-found-land,
My kingdome, safeliest when with one man man'd.

John Donne

ADIEU, I KISS YOU IN THE PLACE WHERE I WILL KISS YOU, WHERE I WANTED TO;
I PLACE MY MOUTH THERE. I ROLL ON YOU. A THOUSAND KISSES.
OH, GIVE ME SOME! GIVE ME SOME!

Gustave Flaubert to Louise Colet

·51·

The Innocent Lover

a delicate inquiry

This is to let you know that all I ask is to be able to hold your hand, and for us to be alone and quiet, together. I want to look into your eyes and read what's in your soul.

If you could love me, the way I love you, how could we be anything else but happy? You are for me like a source of pure air, a branch of white blossoms, a clear stream reflecting a pale sunrise. Truly, you are as delicate as doves and a kind word from you is as precious as a pearl to me.

Yours, happy in the knowledge that your much-loved eyes will read what this hand is now writing.

May all my Hopes of Happiness prove vain if I have any sinister Designs in my Addresses to you; if all my Thoughts of you are not as chaste as Vows of Vestal Virgins at the Altar.

The Amorous Gallant's Tongue

My heart

dropped

as gently

as a leaf

into your
letter

The Star-Crossed Lover

I am haunted by the kiss in your eyes, the kiss you can't give me. Your family disapproves of me, and so do your friends. They will probably never approve of me, but in the end they are going to admire my strength and my faithfulness. They are going to realize that I will never, never give up on you, no matter how hard they make it for us to be together. One day, they will understand that this kind of love, in itself, deserves to be returned.

When I am in bed, about to sleep, or when I'm alone with my thoughts, suddenly I meet your face, and I know you're the one for me, no matter what stands between us.

I love you more *because* I have to fight for you. Write! So I can at least hear your voice on paper, even though I cannot hold you in my arms.

The Lucky Lover

I want to thank you for writing to me. It keeps me alive. When I opened your envelope this morning, I found something so sweet and beautiful that I didn't know what to do — so I cried over it! How can you write such words to me? How can I deserve them? If I'd dreamed of you, I would have chastised myself for such a greedy fantasy.

My heart dropped as gently as a fallen leaf into your letter.

You have led me somewhere I could never have found for myself. I can't believe you've been given to me. You make me feel as if the world was made for me and I can do anything with it. And all day I do nothing, because I can do everything. I feel as if I have found the one diamond left in a big empty mine.

You contain all the sweetness of flowers, soft winds, the sun – the essence of everything I want.

Without you, I couldn't taste sourness of apples, the tartness of red wine, the pearliness of persimmons, without crying. Without you, I'd have to leave my poems on strangers' doorsteps. Without you, every day would be Monday.

Without you, there'd be no point in anything. Don't let there be any time without you, ever, my love.

I am one of God's most fortunate creatures, for not only am I happy, but *I know it!*

You are the one luxury I'll always be able to afford.

The Rose-Tinted Lover
a celebration

I crushed these rose petals (enclosed) in my own hands, which still smell of their perfume, as I write. Last night I watched the Spanish film *Matador*. Have you seen it? It has the most painfully wonderful scene where the lovers roll on rose petals and then he takes a rosebud by the stem in his mouth and he kisses her all over her whole body *with the rose*. It is the most beautiful visual, tactile and perfumed reconciliation of romance and eroticism – the symbol, the smell, the feeling altogether. I *whimpered*.

Like no one before or since, I carry your heart in my heart. You're inside me like my own pulse. A word, a rustle of your dress, a hint of your fragrance, are all it takes to throw me into ecstasy.

e.e. cummings says it the way I would like to say it. One day I'd like to read this poem aloud to you.

Please, with your small hands, answer this letter, which I send to you with a love that carries seasons of rain and roses.

·53·

> somewhere i have never travelled,gladly beyond
> any experience, your eyes have their silence:
> in your most frail gesture are things which enclose me,
> or which i can't touch because they are too near
>
> your slightest look easily will unclose me
> though i have closed myself as fingers,
> you open always petal by petal myself as Spring opens
> (touching skilfully,mysteriously)her first rose
>
> or if your wish be to close me,i and
> my life will shut very beautifully,suddenly,
> as when the heart of this flower imagines
> the snow carefully everywhere descending;
>
> nothing which we are to perceive in this world equals
> the power of your intense fragility:whose texture
> compels me with the colour of its countries
> rendering death and forever with each breathing
>
> (i do not know what it is about you that closes
> and opens;only something in me understands
> the voice of your eyes is deeper than all roses)
> nobody,not even the rain, has such small hands

The Nostalgic Lover
an invitation to remember...

W hat a luxury of bliss we were enjoying a week ago! I remember a hundred dark places we lay in fifty odd remembered times. There's an old-fashioned word to describe what happens to me – I *languish* when I think of you – I languish with sweet joys and memories of the minutes and hours we have spent together. This feeling is so intense that I can almost taste it.

Where are you at this moment? What are you doing? What are you thinking? Can you feel my thoughts enfolding you? Can you remember what I remember, and live it with me? In the midst of this distance from you, I feel only my closeness to you.

Could we ever go back to that forest where I first said "I love you"? Of course, we can. I could find my way back there, blindfolded, with my hands tied behind my back. I can, and will find again all those places I have been with you. I love all those places, and others too, even that horrible café at the railway station, or the supermarket where we met. All these places have a kind of love-magic. I love them because they remind me of you.

I can't forget you for a single instant. Do I love you so much more than you love me or do you, too, feel like this?

·54·

Everything I do, and everything I dream includes you, as wine must

The Inspired Lover

It isn't easy to describe the change you've made in me. But let me try.

Should I telephone you? No, I'll write.

When I am with you I feel that I have been stolen away from a windowless jail-cell and taken to a mountain peak covered in wild flowers. I feel breathless, astonished, and I can see for miles. Last week, I was emotionally embedded in cement; now I'm dancing on the petal's edge, dizzy with aromatic fumes and bouncing on velvet.

I have more to say when I am around you. I think more interesting thoughts. Meanwhile, I watch you expand and blossom underneath my loving eyes. Can't you already feel those mysterious things inside you? More capabilities, higher aspirations, better hopes of life? We imitate the good things in each other, and discard everything else. You are a prism, refracting my life into a rainbow.

·55·

Before I met you, I was quite happy, professionally, and with my family and friends. I was not needy. But then you came into my life and changed everything. I've even been magically released from any need for dentists, accountants, shop assistants, everyone who isn't you.

I wish I had written this poem: it reminds me of us. You plant poems inside me, when you rain your fertile kisses on my face.

I couldn't resist phoning you, after all. You know what I said. Now I long for you.

I think of you.
Your soul streaming into
the morning like a white flame.
Your hair on fire with the sun.
Your veins pulsing wild colors
into the palette of your creativity.

I watch you walking miracles
in my life. Each step baptizing me
with your understanding.
Shining seeds fall from your fingers
into the letters you pen to me.
Until my hungry gaze that eats your words
germinates with seedling stars.
And you become the angel who
stands at the door of my own knowing.
Stephanie June Sorréll

taste of its own grapes. (Adapted from a poem by Elizabeth Barrett Browning.)

The Dreaming Lover

I spend most of my time with my eyes shut, dreaming of you — lovely little cameos of you flitting past, and full-length feature films. I remember things you said, and sweet things you did. I can spend hours like this — eating lotuses, smelling poppies — hours I can hardly believe have passed.

I went to a concert tonight, but the music heightened my emotions to such a pitch that I had to walk out, and go to a bar. A bad idea: every other person was there with their lover. Only I was alone, a solitary Adam before the creation of Eve. Except I wasn't in Paradise. Far from it. I caught your reflection in the mirror. Even the beer bubbled with your humor, the way your face lights up when you laugh. That bar was haunted by you — I had to leave.

When I got home, I sat for a long time in the dark, wanting you, thinking hollow thoughts, containing only your absence. There must be much more empty space in my head than I ever thought! I am going to bed now, so I can dream of you.

To make sure I do, the last thing I'll do is kiss your letter, and wrap my empty arms around the idea of you, and fall fast asleep. Holding on to my fantasy of you, I'll feel that with each breath something leaves me, and goes to you. And there I'll conjure up your face across a candlelit table, holding hands walking down a street in Barcelona at midnight, your wet skin touching mine on an abandoned beach in Haiti. In my dreams, we are the lovers that *others* gaze on enviously.

Why are our pleasures so short and interrupted, and our absences so long and unbroken?

If you are the dreamer,
I am what you dream.
But when you want to wake,
I am your wish ...

Rainer Maria Rilke

"I am lost in love's labyrinth."

Suggested reply: A ball of string, gift-wrapped in a map with arrows to the lover's door

The Delirious Lover
a bacchanalia

I am in love. I am in love. It hangs around me like Zorro's cape – ravishing, swirling, all-embracing. I brandish my beautiful, dangerous sword: it is your love that protects me.

The accounts are undone. There are rainbows in the soapsuds. The butter glows like a candle. The computer hums snatches of Mahler. The bus jerks to erotic rhythms. I fall out at my stop, rubbing my eyes, deliriously spent.

Nothing is quite the same as it was.

I carry your written kisses in my briefcase. They escape at all the wrong moments – in meetings, in the elevator, in the supermarket, and my hands carry them to my lips. I kiss them, I kiss them. (Has a love letter ever been kissed to *dust* before?)

Everything has your name on it. That flower is called "You", because it is so gorgeous. That chair is called "You", because it is so comfortable. I have eyes because I see you. I have lips because they say your name and kiss you.

Everything you do arouses me, terrifies me, tortures me, elates me; everything you do is perfect. You give yourself to me and you reserve nothing.

I love you to infinity, till Friday. Long strings of kisses and caresses bind me to you, shivering, until then. Meanwhile, I'm indulging my imagination – and smiling like a crocodile every time I think of you.

SHORT VERSION

Excuse me for troubling you.
I left my sweater, one of my socks,
some hairs, my heart and my mind
at your house last night
I shall soon be completely naked ...

The Thirsty Lover

I am sitting in the bar writing this. I started at the Sir Francis Drake, and I will do a tour of duty in all the great bars of this city before morning. There's a storm outside, a fresh wind and a choppy sea for my voyage. But the earth isn't big enough for me tonight. I am now at The Globe and plan to proceed to The Moon and Stars, and then make a journey to all the planets, ending in the constellation of Venus – anything so as to be closer to the pleasure zone that is yours, all yours.

It's not my fault that I am here. It *would* start to rain as we were waiting for the bus, and those stupid friends of mine, hauled me into this bar. It is a dark, cold, confounded hole, fit only for desperadoes and down-and-outs. The cold outside made the warmth of the wine work faster on me.

I wish you could see me now as I am definitely not myself any more. I'm a much pleasanter, warmer, wittier person than when cold sober and I am sure that I could win your love when I am like this.

The wine hisses upon my heart. Cupid has fired a dart into my liver. I am asking the barman for ice to cool my fevered thoughts. Ice! Clear and cold, and definitely melting, just like you. The idiot has brought me olives instead. This is a damnable place. A hideous world. I wish I was out of it, in heaven, by which, of course, I mean in your arms. Ah, if only they were bottling your bath water – *then* there'd be something to slake this incredible thirst! I'd close my eyes, sip you slowly, and let you slide down my throat.

This is my constant prayer, whether I am drunk or sober.

Farewell. I am sure I shall write to you again tomorrow to apologize for this letter. (Adapted from a letter in an 18th-century manual.)

Goodnight, my love. How I wish I was in the corner of your fireplace to warm up your soup.

Henri IV of France to Corisande d'Andoins, Comtess de Guiche

The Hungry Lover
an invitation to delectation

I would like to fill your supermarket trolley to overflowing. I want to reach deep into your freezer cabinets and close my fingers round your ripest strawberries. I want to melt your cool dairy products in my hot hands. I wish to rummage long and deep in your confectionery counter. I want to lay waste to your delicatessen department. I want to take advantage of your special offer. **And when we get home, I want to tear off your packaging immediately.**

ALTERNATIVE SHORT VERSION

Feeling peckish. Would like a letter to chew on. Would like a chocolate malted milkshake. Would like you here. Would like a lemon meringue pie and pinkly cooked leg of lamb with rosemary and garlic. Would like you here. Would like some love. Feeling greedy.

I EMBRACE YOU. I KISS YOU. I FEEL WILD.
WERE YOU HERE, I'D BITE YOU:
I LONG TO DO SO ... YES, I FEEL WITHIN ME NOW
THE APPETITES OF WILD BEASTS,
THE INSTINCTS OF A LOVE THAT IS CARNIVOROUS ...
Gustave Flaubert to Louise Colet

You delicious morsel of edible sensuality ... I could eat you!

·59·

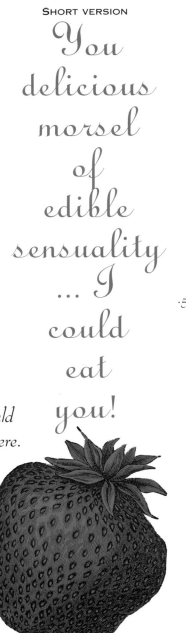

The Frustrated Lover

I wish you were here, and not there. If you were here, writing love letters would be the last thing on my mind.

·60·

APHRODISIAC

I'm wearing your kiss, the last one I tore from your lips – more vivid than a scar.

I want my mouth to melt into your mouth. I want to feel your heart beating next to mine. I want to crush you in my arms until you almost break and then to stroke you tenderly all over. I want to face you, hold your knees in mine. The smell of you lingers on my pillow. I found your hairpin in my bed – it has become my dark fetish, my irreplaceable memento of your sweet, disordered hair.

I can't get enough of you. Give me that kiss I taught you, that delicious night, that position we invented, that infinitely tender caress with which you last left me. Gather me up in your arms and let me press my flesh entirely against yours. Wake me up every hour with more demands for love.

This paper love is nothing. The real thing is pulsing in my bones and my nerves, tormenting me like a grain of sand in this empty bed.

Write to me without your clothes on and let the letter touch your whole body before you send it to me. And I will do anything you ask of me, with delight.

Is there any antidote to the fatal aphrodisiac which is you?

ALTERNATIVE SHORT VERSION:

Of course, if one was noble enough, then just loving would be as good as seeing, tasting, touching, kissing, holding. But oh! I am not noble enough! I need to caress you with melodious strokes outside, inside Everywhere ··

The Clandestine Lover

an invitation to indiscretion

It's agony to hide what I feel for you, and last night was the worst torture. I am starting to be teased about you. Little comments have been made, and last night, one or two horrible people watched my eyes the whole evening and would not let me send you a single loving glance, and to disappoint everyone I was forced to make much fuss of and flirt with X. But you must be crazy to think someone else, especially X, could take your place.

No matter how dangerous this liaison becomes, I can't give up the happiness you mean to me. Even if you were married three times over and had ten children and six cats, I would still feel that I had more right to you than anyone else on earth.

If you are suffering as much as I am, then I am sorry for you. I need to kiss you all over and let myself be kissed all over by you. Come quickly, quickly. My heart will *break*.

The Midnight Lover

• MIDNIGHT PRODUCTIONS •
THE ISLANDS

FAX SHEET

Date: _____ Time: _____

To: Oberon Phone: _____
Fax: _____

From: Titania Phone: _____
Fax: _____

Re: Midsummer Night

cc: Bottom

Number of pages including cover sheet: 1

Message

Meet you tonight
Same place as last time.
Don't bring Puck. He'll only get in the way.

SHORT VERSION

I don't just want to sleep with you. That's the wrong word, entirely. I want to be awake with you, kissing your kisses back and stroking your fluttering fingers as they caress me.

The Satisfied Lover

Darling, I have your letter, which is as sweet as honey on my tongue. I found this poem by Rabindranath Tagore. It expresses some of what I feel for you, though not everything. The rest I will whisper into your own much-loved ear with my arms around you. I know you'll appreciate all the resonances of this poem. I'm grateful for knowing you, because you will.

Your veil of the saffron color makes my eyes drunk.
The jasmine wreath that you wove thrills to my heart like praise.
It is a game of giving and withholding, revealing and
screening again; some smiles and some little shyness,
and some sweet useless struggles.
This love between you and me is as simple as a song.

No mystery beyond the present; no striving for the
impossible; no shadow behind the charm; no groping
in the depth of the dark.
This love between you and me is as simple as a song.

We do not stray out of all words into the ever silent;
We do not raise our hands to the void for things beyond hope.
It is enough what we give and we get.
We have not crushed the joy to the utmost to wring from it the wine of pain.
This love between you and me is as simple as a song.

I'm luxuriating in your letter like an expertly stroked cat.

The Country Lover
a rustic invitation

Let's go to the country and consecrate the fields. I want to be in your hot, tanned arms in the open air. I want to rustle the hay and the shake the grass out of your hair.

The return of the fine weather has led me to form a vague wish that we might vagabondize one day in the country — before the summer is clear gone. I love the country and like to leave certain associations in my memory, which seem, as it were, the land marks of affection — Am I very obscure?

Mary Wollstonecraft to Gilbert Imlay

The Urban Lover
a postcard sequence

Do you know what I love most? It's walking along the street with you, when you can't resist putting your hand on my back, my arm, my hip — those little touches that only lovers give, that give away everything.

I walk this street against the crowds that push towards me, and by selecting the features that pass, I try to form a synthesis of your face. You are not there.

Based on a letter by
Vita Sackville-West

Many thoughts of you, but never the right moment to set them down in a letter. They are safe, though, and will follow later.

The Cultural Lover
the travel temptation

Do you remember all our departures – how we huddled together under the terminus clocks, and how the car crunched on the damp gravel as we drove out from small hotels at dawn?

Hand in hand, soul with soul, we had no sense of anything that was not our love. And when we arrived at our destinations, and when we visited cathedrals and museums and galleries, we admired everything through a prism of emotion that made a rainbow in our hearts. Together we prowled piazzas and café lattes under our own private sun.

How often have we heard the train whispering "*How* I love you, *How* I love you, *How* I love you," as it carried us along. How many masterpieces have inspired me because you loved them, and because you could explain their mysteries to me? How many staircases have I climbed to the top of, how many interminable campanili because you were walking up them ahead of me?

Not enough, my darling. Signed with an exotic, far-away kiss ...

(Inspired by a letter from Juliette Drouet.)

HOW I love you

For me, dearest love, there are twenty three sacred towns. They are Neuchâtel, Geneva, Vienna, St. Petersburg, Dresden, Cannstadt, Karlsruhe, Strasbourg, Passy, Fontainebleau, Orléans, Bourges, Tours, Blois, Paris, Rotterdam, The Hague, Antwerp, Brussels, Baden, Lyons, Toulon, Naples. I do not know what they mean to you but for me, when one of these names enters my thoughts, it is as if a Chopin were touching a piano key; sounds reverberate through my soul, and a complete poem takes shape.

Neuchâtel is like a white lily, pure, filled with pervasive scents; youth, freshness, excitement, hope, fleetingly perceived happiness. Geneva is the passion of dreams, the kind of dream where life is flashed before one ...Vienna is mourning in the midst of joy ... And St. Petersburg? What a union: it lasted for two months without a false note, unless one is to count that argument over the hat and the one about the expense of engaging a cook ... But Lyons! oh! Lyons, showed me my love transcended by a charm, a tenderness, a perfect quality of caresses and a loving gentleness which makes Lyons for me one of those shibboleths special in a man's life, and which, when spoken, are like the holy word with which a man may open the path to heaven! ... A thousand embraces to remind us of our twenty three towns.

Honoré de Balzac to Countess Evelina Hanska

The Horticultural Lover
an invitation to the garden

You remind me of a secret garden ... your vivid blossoms open in my heart, your intoxicating fragrance stirs me, your mysterious paths beckon, irresistibly. Distant birdsong calls me to scale your high walls.

It pains me to see such beauty untended ... I have green fingers, and I'm told that there there might be a position vacant for a head gardener?

I have just been gardening, beloved ... My eyes were as moist as my flowers, but I was not weeping. While I busied myself with the garden, I reviewed in thought the lovely flowers of my past happiness. I saw them again fresh and blooming as the first day, and I felt close to you, separated only by a breath ... I should have liked to pluck my soul and send it to you as a nosegay.

Juliette Drouet to Victor Hugo

HOW I love you, HOW I love you.

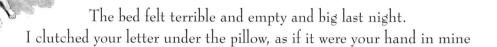

The Separated Lover

SHORT VERSIONS

The bed felt terrible and empty and big last night.
I clutched your letter under the pillow, as if it were your hand in mine

●

YOU ARE WITH ME EVEN WHEN YOU ARE NOT WITH ME. EVERY TIME
SOMEONE SAYS, "I LOVE YOU" ON TELEVISION, IN A SONG, OR IN A BOOK,
IT THRILLS ME AS IF IT WERE YOUR OWN WORDS TO ME.

●

I'm working on a huge 'Welcome Home' banner for you. The longer you
stay away the more embarrassing it's going to be.

●

 Your face is never out of my
mind. Without you, I am as
lonely as a single earring, as a
widowed swan, as the number 1

●

HERE IS A GREEN LEAF. REMEMBER, I'LL BE BACK BEFORE IT FADES TO
BROWN. REMEMBER, I AM SO WRAPPED IN THOUGHTS OF YOU THAT YOUR
ABSENCE AT THIS MOMENT IS A MERE TECHNICALITY.

●

You have gone. You were able to leave me for three days! No, I shall
never survive so long a separation. It's only been an hour, and
already I can't bear it! I'm never in our lives going to
let us be apart for another night.

(based on a letter by Madame D'Epinay)

Aloe Purpurea Lævis

The Separated Lover
(expanded version)

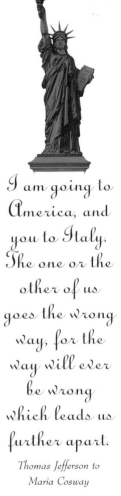

Since you went away I don't sleep any more. I just have periods of exhausted blackness amid a tumult of feelings. As soon as I close my eyes, I am with you, stroking your heart, kissing your eyelids, feeling them flutter under my lips. If I dream, it is of you in some terrible danger. In this dream, only I can protect you. I wake up, turn to you for comfort and find only emptiness. My voice is on your pillow, whispering to you, wherever you are.

I watch the stars rise here, and know the same stars watch you. I listen to the weather report for your part of the country. I see you putting on your grey raincoat, and draping your silk scarf around your neck. No one does it as gracefully as you. I see you on the train. I see you rustling in your old briefcase, looking for my last letter. I see you holding it in your hand as you hurtle across the country, gazing out of the window, thinking of me.

Everyone is being kind, knowing my loneliness, but nothing can make up for the lack of you. I'm incomplete without you. How slow the minutes, how long the hours, how many the miles between us.

You'll be pleased to hear that I spent some time with your parents while you are away. It was one way of feeling close to you, to be with people who love you as much as I do, and who, like me, will never tire of talking about you, wondering how you are.

You'll think I am getting sentimental, or senile, or both, but I also spent last night looking at our holiday photographs and remembering that marvellous week. When we spend nearly every evening together, we tend to forget what a priceless treasure we have in our relationship. It takes little separations like this to make us remember that, and to realize that, like Paradise, you are always both near and far from me.

Darling! I just received your letter. Now I can breathe again. You've taken all the pain out of me. You tell me you love me. You tell me in a way you've never expressed it before. Oh say it again, say it all the time, never stop saying it, so I can believe it anew each time. Then tell me over and over again, for by tomorrow I might begin to doubt again. Never wander more than a thought's breath away from me, from this light we kindle together.

"Lovingly your Livy" — the very dearest words to me that ever illuminated paper & gave it a glory as of a vision. How the words seem to nestle up to me! — & put arms about me, & a loved head upon my shoulder, & the hymning of the angels in my heart!
Mark Twain (Samuel Clemens) to Olivia Langdon

I am going to America, and you to Italy. The one or the other of us goes the wrong way, for the way will ever be wrong which leads us further apart.

Thomas Jefferson to Maria Cosway

The Rational Lover
a request for simplicity

No word from you for four days. But don't expect me to hang myself just because you feel like playing with my heart. It would be very stupid of me to want to leave the world while you, the greatest treasure, are still in it.

Besides, you're no idiot. I know you'd prefer my real, strong voice telling you I love you to a faint, distant echo from the past, and I am sure you would rather have a living lover than some sad, regretted image, slowly blurring with time.

Love is not some kind of melodrama. It is pure pleasure. Or should be, and *has* been, for us. Nor should we descend into a childish mass of wants, dreams, games and tantrums.

My heart is full of love for you. I have no need to dilate or dilute my feelings, or dress them in ceremony. When I write to you, I want to be the lover you recognize, the one you say you already love: I will write to you the way I talk to you, without tricks or treats.

... So, even though you may want to hear it, you are *not* a velvet rose, nor a fern-fringed pond, nor a spangled sunrise, nor the gilded stars at night. To me, you *are* a poem, but I can't write you down in flowery words. I can only write what I know, and therefore I write I love you, and when I say I love you, then it is forever.

Now, tell me, in words as simple as this, do you love me too? Don't hide behind someone else's elegant thoughts. I want to hear it directly from your heart, and in your own voice.

But otherwise beware! If you treat my love carelessly, and leave it for days without attention, then you may not find it when you suddenly decide you want it again.

·68·

The Rapturous Lover
a written kiss

Remember how we kissed last night? How you kissed my eyes? I'm enclosing a poem by Nina Cassian, which expresses exactly what your kisses do to me. Don't you feel it, too? An exquisite thrill in every cell of your body? Only love can do that.

Last night – I remember everything – the firelight flickered shadows on the walls, the curtains suddenly shivered in the breeze, the moonlight escaped through them and touched your face and your fingers locked with mine.

Suddenly, I feel as if nothing but you really reaches deep inside me, and the depths of me are reaching only for you, nothing else, nobody else. In my mind, you and I are on our own island, entirely self-sufficient, living out an uninterrupted continuous act of love. You seemed to have absorbed all the value and all the beauty of anything in the world and made it part of yourself. Every other attractive person seems a mere forgery of you.

I think about, adore, trust, you – only you. I'm like a harp – quiet, until you come and draw your hand across my strings. Then music sings out. I am dazed with excitement. And I long for a clear well of spirit to cleanse my past life, so I can stand beside you without feeling so utterly unworthy.

·69·

Our kisses, hundreds, thousands –
even millions – who knows!
I never counted them:
my fruits, squirrels, carnations, rivers – my knives!
I could sleep and dream on your mouth,
sing and die there, again and again;
that mouth – deep harbour
for a night's lodging after a long journey, reaching it,
yet still longing to reach it ...

They're battles – our kisses –
heavy, slow, hurtful
where blood, voice and memory all take part.
oh how jealous I am of the water you drink
and of the words you speak –
of your blue sighs ...
Jealous of those unjust partings –
of our mouths!

The Fearful Lover

It's a shame that you don't take pleasure in being nice more often, since, when you *are* nice, no one does it better or more deliciously than you.

But you're only sweet to me when I am unhappy. This seems a wicked conundrum: am I supposed to be miserable all the time, just so that you'll be kind? I can't be happy with you, and I can't be happy without you. I try to balance the fear and pain against the joy you give me: but what's the use in counting? I love you.

You have no idea how afraid I am of you. I am more terrified of you than anything in the world — toothache, muggers, cockroaches, thunder, bankruptcy. And you have so many different shapes and sides — the kind, the soft, the hard, the strong. The one that wants me no more than three feet away, and the one that wishes I was on another planet. How can you expect me to change my shape to follow yours, every time?

But believe me, I love you so much that even if you were at least once a week changed in to a dragon, I would find a way to fall in love with your scales and claws and become addicted to fiery kisses. I'm just asking you to be patient, while I catch up with your transformations, and to take pity on me if I get burnt.

In the meantime, I close my eyes and abandon myself to you trustfully, like a blind man to his guide. Show me the way to your heart.

I have spread my dreams under your feet:
Tread softly, because you tread on my dreams.

William Butler Yeats

I could not help feeling how unequal were the heart-riches we might offer each to each: I, for the first time, giving my all at once, and forever ...

Edgar Allan Poe to Sarah Helen Whitman

The Combustible Lover

a conflagration

Y ou set my heart on fire. I love you. I hate you. Whenever I breathe the same air as you, my heart bursts into a million pieces and scatters. The room shrinks and the air grows thick with sparks. Your kisses explode like hand-grenades and your not-given kisses are like bomb-craters.

Forgive me – I can't behave like a normal person when I'm with you. Everything goes up in flames. What do you expect when you keep dropping your lighted matches onto my dry tinder?

What astonishing fireworks we set off together! We could keep the coldest night warm with our burning and light it up with our flaming wonder.

Be careful when you re-seal the envelope – a million kisses will come flying out to wrap themselves around you. Can you hear those kisses detonating? And taste the smell of burning?

Yours, at the end of a very short fuse ...

To feel, to touch your hand of love, that hand full of sweet, proud sensibilities ... that hand polished and soft with love, is a happiness as great as your caress of honey and fire.

·71·

Honoré de Balzac to Countess
Evelina Hanska

The Regular Lover

Lyle Lovett is singing, "I've got the moon on my pillow, and you on my mind." And I'm lying here, thinking of you, and listening to the sea.

Before you read any further, go and put on your silk scarf/blue shirt/old jeans. I want to think of your wearing it/them. Then you are most mine.

I have no news. I have no reason at all to write to you, just like the last five times I wrote to you. Maybe it's just my way of making sure you're thinking of me as often as I'm thinking of you, and so you know that I love you at a quarter to midnight on a Monday night and that I love you eleven and three-quarter hours more than I did this morning. I love the faint soreness in my ribs after a night with you, and the wicked tickle there before I see you. You've imprisoned my heart and I haven't the least desire to rattle the cage.

I found this poem today and it said just what I was thinking.

The Innocence of any flesh sleeping

Sleeping beside you I dreamt
I woke beside you;
waking beside you
I thought I was dreaming.

Have you ever slept beside an ocean?
Well yes,
it is like this.

The whole motion of landscapes, of oceans
is within her.
She is
the innocence of any flesh sleeping,
so vulnerable
no protection is needed.

In such times
the heart opens,
contains all there is,
there being no more than her.

In what country she is
I cannot tell.
But knowing –
because there is love
and it blots out all demons –
she is safe,
I can turn,
sleep well beside her.

Waking beside her I am dreaming.
Dreaming of such wakings
I am to all love's senses woken.

Brian Patten

The Endless Lover

I want to love you every way a person can be loved – properly, improperly, devilishly, angelically, wildly, gently.

I love the way you always hold me tighter when I say it's time to go. I love the way your heart gallops audibly when you're in my arms. I love the way I always hear something tearing when we part.

And I love *you* the way the waves love the shore, the way the nightingale loves the moon, the way cinnamon loves warm bread, the way God loves the wicked, the way the grape loves the winepress, the way a sunflower loves the sun.

I'll never get to the end of this letter. With every word I write I love you more, and then I need to describe it ... So write to *me*. Anything. Even a single line. But tell me that you love me. Just those three words would be enough: for me, they are everything.

(Inspired by letters from George Bernard Shaw and Mark Twain.)

Love can read the writing on the remotest star ...

Oscar Wilde to
Lord Alfred
Douglas

·73·

I AM BUILDING YOU THE

You always
surprise me. Your last kiss is always
the sweetest thing I ever tasted; your last word the
wittiest; your last smile the most radiant.

You don't know it but I watched you sleeping last night, and I could
not believe that there could be such beauty in my own bed, calm and
trusting, and seeming to feel it belonged there. I covered your shoulder with
the sheet, and waited patiently until you woke up, so I could kiss you.

You don't know it, but I watched you walking down our street yesterday and I was filled
with a shock of desire and delight, as if I had only then seen you for the first time.

The Surprised Lover

You can't know it, but just now I tucked your morning love-letter behind your photograph
on the mantelpiece, so I can look up often and see the two things I love best in this room,
side by side.

In the photograph you're wearing a white shirt and an old leather belt. There's that
quality of innocence and trust, that slight knowing curve to your lips, as if you
know I am looking at you know, as if you know I'm talking to your
photograph, and telling it how much I love you, I love you, I love you.

Mary Chapin Carpenter is singing "Passionate Kisses" as I write.

Many of those to you, sweetheart.

(Inspired by a letter from John Keats.)

PEDESTAL OF YOUR CHOICE

The Familiar Lover

When I first met you, I learnt to drink double expresso with five sugars so we could share one cup. You were like bitter-sweet marmalade, sharp balsamic vinegar, pungent spices, fiery brandy. Your piquant kisses burnt my mouth. But now, my darling, you taste like warm bread and honey – sweet, soft, familiar – and completely nourishing.

The Comforting Lover

Deeply Beloved,
I understand how you are hurting. I can feel it under my own skin. You don't need to be pretend to be strong just to make me happy. Your concerns are my concerns, your losses are my grief.

I want to help without needing to be asked. I may not have the solution, but I do want to listen.

I simply *live* on the love your letters bring and I hope this one of mine is strong enough to carry something back to you to help you feel safer, more loved, stronger, better. Remember, I have a store of belief in you that can never be exhausted. Remember how proud I am that you are mine.

Tell me you love me. I already see your poor sad lips shaped to say the word "love". They are *so* kissable then. Let me kiss away your pain, and then you can rest in my arms.

Until then, put this letter in your heart and it will help the hurt to go away. Remember that while we love each other there is still something beautiful in this troubled world.

The Neglected Lover
a request for consideration

I hope you'll find time to open this letter. Perhaps it's the only way I can tempt you to pay me some attention, because you can barely bear to take your eyes and hands away from your new kitten/car/computer/mobile phone/job.

You are *everything* to me. So I am sorry, but I just can't share your total devotion to ... I 'm a living, breathing person, and I can't deal with being virtually ignored for this non-human object. What about me? I'm as close to you as your own shadow! I love you more than my own skin! There's scarcely any room for kittens/cars/computers/mobile phones/jobs.

Let me reason with you. What's so special about ...? How has it come to monopolize your attention? While I languish here, lonely and uncaressed, you are pouring your whole soul into it.

Please try to look at us in the same light: What does x have which I do not? What qualifies it to receive all your love? And does it pine for your affection the way I do? Can it make love to you the way I do? Do you share the same in-jokes, the same Sunday mornings in bed, the same love of 1940s movies? Do you prefer it because it does not wear herringbone socks? (I would be happy to take mine off, if that is what it takes to get your attention.)

Does it bring you flowers and cups of coffee for no reason at all? Does it write you love letters?

Go ahead, compare us. Is ... better looking than I am? Even if you think that's the case, which of us is the more intelligent and amusing? Which, in the long run, is better company? *Exactly*.

I am prepared for a duel with ... for your attention. Or whatever it is that will make you come back to me, forsaking ... completely, or at least during hours that should be ours alone.

I am writing this letter with my tongue in my cheek, as the saying goes, but I want you to know I am hurt and I want to sort this out before it gets *really* serious. Maybe you are expressing your love for me by working hard, but if that's the case, I want you to tell me so.

Yours, but not unconditionally ...

Where have you gone? Where do butterflies go when it snows?

The Endearing Lover

My Harley Davidson, my leather-bound Filofax, my Italian gelato, my mobile phone, my Hermès scarf, my Prada wallet, my First Night ticket at the Met, my Tuscan sun-dried tomato, my glass of Sauternes with my thick tranche of foie gras, my rough-hewn chocolate truffle, my honeyed insomnia, my mad middle-of-the-night, my extra-dry Martini, my expensive orchid, my extravagant Valentine, my neon sign spelling "Love", my first thought in the morning, my last sigh at night, my enchanted trysting place, my duelling revolver, my first snowdrop, my final gasp, my good fight in a just cause, my clover to roll in, my luscious crushed apricot in my glass of champagne, my blushing peach, the fragrant mango juice dribbling down my chin, my drop of dew, my miracle drug, my point of no return, my fresh fortune cookie, my single rose, my dozen oysters, my small bird singing afar in a lost land, my hummable melody, my hurried feast, my plume in my aunt's hat, my strawberries glistening with sugar, my stars above the desert night, the snow on my minaret ...what a tragedy it is to be alone in bed when you are alive!

The Vintage Lover

I am 56 years old. You are 23. This is a great *contrast*, but perhaps the *difference* between us is simply in the numbers?

But how can I ask you to love someone of my age? I'm not going to ask for miracles. All I can really ask of you is to regret that I am older and to wish that I were younger – I think I would be happy with that. The gift of a wish is a small thing – please, don't refuse it. Be as sweet and generous as I know you are.

When you know me better, I'm sure that the greyness of my hair will be irrelevant because of the greenness of my affection for you. Loving you takes years off me. You will find me a young lover, though you may think of me as an older man.

My love will be more sincere and unchanging than that of young people, who are still playing the field, afraid to commit. Do you really want just half of someone's wandering heart, when you can have all of mine? My age makes me unselfish in my love for you. For goodness sake, I love everyone who loves you. Even the other young people who want your attentions.

And I can offer you one thing more: I will try harder.

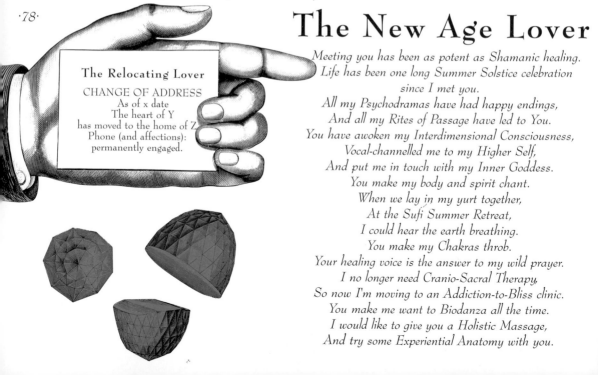

The Relocating Lover

CHANGE OF ADDRESS
As of x date
The heart of Y
has moved to the home of Z
Phone (and affections):
permanently engaged.

The New Age Lover

Meeting you has been as potent as Shamanic healing.
Life has been one long Summer Solstice celebration
since I met you.
All my Psychodramas have had happy endings,
And all my Rites of Passage have led to You.
You have awoken my Interdimensional Consciousness,
Vocal-channelled me to my Higher Self,
And put me in touch with my Inner Goddess.
You make my body and spirit chant.
When we lay in my yurt together,
At the Sufi Summer Retreat,
I could hear the earth breathing.
You make my Chakras throb.
Your healing voice is the answer to my wild prayer.
I no longer need Cranio-Sacral Therapy,
So now I'm moving to an Addiction-to-Bliss clinic.
You make me want to Biodanza all the time.
I would like to give you a Holistic Massage,
And try some Experiential Anatomy with you.

The Pre-Nuptual Lover

We keep joking about getting married, but it's time to get serious about it now. We've grown up a lot in the last few months and what we have is so good that I don't want to take the chance of it fading away. We are at that point where we are so cosy together that I am afraid that you will get bored, or that the thrill of a new romance might distract you. You're so attractive, people are bound to keep falling for you ... so I'm asking you to marry me now.

Our romance and our passion, though memorable and exciting will, in the end, have no meaning unless we seal it with a commitment to each other. Otherwise, this relationship has been just one long, very enjoyable, job interview without securing the job. And that's not what either of us intended. Ever since I met you I have been looking on each day we spend together as a investment in this hope for our happiness together.

I have known you for two years. Two blissful years. During all that time my opinion of you has never wavered, but gone on increasing in love and respect.

Regarding the timing, well, as you know, my annual leave is in December, which would give us time to plan ... so I would like to be married just before Christmas. It will be cold outside, but lovers like us don't need to go out of doors very much. Perhaps I also want to show you how cheerful and cosy we can make a home of our own. I also want to be married in the winter, because it will take us many long nights together to say all that we have to say to each other.

Whatever will give you pleasure by way of a ceremony and honeymoon will be my pleasure too, and I want to make sure that we have an occasion that also bonds our families together.

If I did not think I could make you happy, I would not ask you to marry me. My heart is warm for you – warmer than any nest.

My sweet Morsel of Modesty, you can't tell how much I love,

nor can I well tell myself; but it is very sincerely;

for I protest to make you the Mistress of my Thoughts, and the Lady of my Returns,

·79·

and commit all my Moveables into your Hands: and to confirm it,

I give you an earnest Kiss in the high Road of Matrimony.

The Amorous Gallant's Tongue

The Organized Lover

Dearest,

I am asking you to give your life to me for safe-keeping, and so, to be fair, I'm sitting here reckoning up what I can offer in return. Here is the estate, which will be *All Yours* if you will agree to be *All Mine*.

1.) A copy of John Donne's love poems, much tattered and abused, but every one about you.

2.) A stack of Simon & Garfunkel CDs.

3.) A ribbon-bound pile of love letters from a fascinating person who seems to love me.

4.) A whole science of kisses – liquid, solid, melting, transpiring.

5.) An old pocket knife.

6.) Scrupulous punctuality and total faithfulness.

7.) The remote control to my TV.

8.) My heart.

Can you accept these things in return for your whole life?

The Divorced or Widowed Lover

I have been alone for some time now. I thought I had learned to enjoy reflected light, from my children, from my friends. But since I met you, I feel the stirring of something alive inside me, still yearning towards a light all of my own.

I found that light in you, unexpectedly, when we met, and everything we have done together since has only made it shine stronger.

I've also been thinking how wonderful it would be if my children could have the friendship of a mature person who cares about them, knows how to show affection, approval and disapproval. I would love to share some of these joys and responsibilities with you. My children are kind and good people, and would welcome you into their hearts and lives, as I would into mine.

You don't need to worry about ... (former partner). I still miss him/her and no one will ever fill the exact gap he/she has left in all our lives. But you have created your own unique and special niche in my heart. I want you to be there, always.

The Story-Telling Lover

an alternative proposal

ONCE UPON A TIME there was a cynical and slightly jaded woman who'd had her share of love affairs, including one quite serious one, but she was tired of the pain of breaking up and had almost decided to give up the idea of love altogether.

She devoted herself to business and to friends and family, and was enjoying a full and happy life. It was, however, without any of the real highs, or deep lows that make for a rich existence.

Then one day she met an extraordinary man. He liked skiing in Italy and 14th-century Siennese painters. So did she. He liked walks in the wild and Sunday mornings in the city. So did she. He loved Purcell and Praetorius, but also Clapton and Dylan. So did she. They had days that danced. Their nights vibrated. Their mornings shimmered. They felt just a little lower than the angels.

After they had spent some months together, as a kind of couple, nothing formal, no real arrangements nor commitment, the woman began to realize that this was something that she wanted to have forever. And she started to look at her work and her life in a different way, and found there was a vacancy for another person to share in everything. She decided to ask the man to come to live with her. She put the idea in a letter, which she wrote as if it was a kind of fairy story, because this was how her life had seemed since she met him.

This story is to be published as a part work and the final instalment is to be his answer to the letter.

Please submit your manuscript as soon as possible. There is a deadline.

... for my sake, sweet, let the few years go by; we are married, and my arms are round you, and my face touches yours, and I am asking you, 'Were you not to me, in that dim beginning of 1846, a joy behind all joys, a life added to and transforming mine, the good I choose from all the possible gifts of God on this earth, for which I seemed to have lived ...'

Robert Browning to
Elizabeth Barrett

·81·

The Accepting Lover

Your letter was the most beautiful compliment I've ever received. Even if I weren't already head over heels in love with you, I would be, after reading your letter.

As for your proposal, I would promise to think about it, but what would be the use? You have evidently made up your mind.

You have made me very happy. I try to think rationally about the big step we are taking, but I can hardly hear my brain for the beating of my heart. I accept your love as freely as it is given, and all of mine is yours in return.

I have no fears for our future so long as you are with me. In case you are still in suspense, *of course* I will marry you and I will love you forever. I can't wait until you're home and we can start planning our life together. I found this poem the other day and it made me think of you and long for you. This marriage idea makes me feel as if we're falling in love all over again – it feels so fresh and new.

The First Marriage

imagine the very first marriage a girl
and boy trembling with some inchoate
need for ceremony a desire for witness:
inventing formality like a wheel or a hoe

in a lost language in a clearing too far from here
a prophet or prophetess intoned to the lovers
who knelt with their hearts cresting
like the unnamed ocean thinking This is true

thinking they will never be alone again
though planets slip their tracks and fish
desert the sea repeating those magic sounds
meaning I do: on this stone below
this tree before these friends yes in body
and word my darkdream my sunsong yes I do I do

Peter Meinke

The Newly Married Lover

My Darling Wife/Husband,

How wonderful it is to be able to use that word – wife/husband – what a difference one little word can make!

Did you think that just because we're now sharing the same bed, I'd give up the joy of writing you love letters? We've barely been apart for a few hours since we married, but all those hours are taken up with thoughts of you.

I love the security of knowing your routine, being able to picture everything you are doing. I used to be stimulated by work and travel, but now I find the biggest thrill is in this thing that we are building together, privately, in our own house – a marriage, a love, a family. Suddenly, home, the safest place on earth, is also the most exciting.

I want to tell you how privileged I feel to be married to you. I feel so safe with you. There is no shadow of doubt, no fear, no loss.

Now that we have found each other, and made sure of each other, let us hold on to that, and make a dazzlingly beautiful life together.

The Multiplying Lover

I can hardly believe we have reproduced ourselves, and our love, so perfectly. I have never seen anything so beautiful or so moving as my first glimpse of you with our son/daughter in your arms – tired, triumphant, proud – *mine*.

This baby is the seal on our happiness – our love made real – a living symbol of our joy in each other. So, let's always be lovers as well as parents. I can't think of a better example to set for our child.

I see you as my young wife, then a young mother, but always the same, always my Adèle, as tender, as adored in the chastity of married life as in the virgin days of your first love ...

Victor Hugo to
Adèle Foucher

·83·

I reckon upon your love as something that is to endure when everything than can perish has perished ...

Nathaniel Hawthorne to Sophia Peabody, his future wife

The Anniversary Lover

For ... years, I have lived in the Paradise of your love.

Tonight we shall have a party and celebrate in public all our decades together. But I want to write you a private love letter first, one to add to that old, ribboned heap from the first years of our relationship. I know you have kept all my letters. And I, of course, would never be parted from yours.

To the fresh, innocent feelings of those early days, I can now add layers and layers of mature love. We have been through so much together. My faith is built on you. It's a fine and solid structure.

Tenderly, we have watched each other grow professionally. We have created and nurtured our children together, we have loved each other's changing faces and we have never let our love get lost in the mediocrity of everyday life. No one compares to you. No one could replace you in my heart. Every morning, when I wake up, I still look first to make sure you are there, and I am always grateful. I love the way you still drop everything to give me a kiss every time I come home, and you still reach for my hand when the lights go down at the movies.

Tonight we will have many witnesses to the union of these hearts, which age has not withered, nor the passing of time cooled towards each other.

There will be family rituals and speeches. But nothing is more important than what I have to say to you: I love you.

I wish sometimes that I could marry you once a year, just to have that moment of solemnity, that breathless, frightening, holy feeling of total commitment to another person. Since I can't do that, I rededicate myself to you today, now and forever. Take these simple flowers, the same violets I always give you on our anniversary. Know that I picked them for you. If there ever comes any anniversary when I do not offer you such a gift then I shall no longer be on this earth.

Happy Anniversary, my love.

DENOUEMENTS · AND · CODAS ·

·85·

The Querulous Lover
a reproach

You rarely make the time to see me and when you do, it's only to tease and play with my feelings. I've made it my business to please you, to love you, to help you. If having a joke at my expense is one more service I can add to this list, then by all means go ahead. But please understand that while this may be a little thing to you, it is a big thing to me.

Tell me it's not true, but this is how it *seems* to me: you've only been pretending to love me, but all the while you've had another agenda. Or is it that you're simply too skilled at love? Look how you seduced me. How you said you would lie on my doorstep all night. How you pushed roses through my letterbox. How you told me that I was an angel in your eyes. But from the moment I gave you my love and my trust, you seemed to lose interest. Please tell me I'm wrong.

I don't think I've ever met anyone so confusing or so desirable. You're tearing me apart. I know that somewhere in there is the sweet and compassionate person I love, who loves me, and who would never willingly inflict pain on their adoring lover.

♥

Still so bright, still so malicious, so skilful, in presenting good from a false side, so unmerciful, to laugh at a sufferer, to ridicule one who complains, all these amiable cruelties are contained in your letter ...
Johann Wolfgang von Goethe to Kaetchen Schoenkopf

♥

I take my pen again to tell you that I am at your knees, that I still love you, that I detest you sometimes, that the day before yesterday I said horrible things about you, that I kiss your beautiful hands, that I kiss them again pending something better, that I am at the end of my tether, that you are divine, etc.

Alexander Pushkin to Anna Petrovna Kern

·86·

The Jealous Lover
an appeal for reassurance

You're probably surprised to have this letter from me, instead of a telephone call, or me hurtling into your arms, as usual. But I can't bring myself to confront you in person. I have good reason to believe that you may not want my company, nor my voice.

I've always opened my heart to you freely and sincerely and I ask you to do the same. Even though I love you, and respect you, I do know that all of us are not as good, all the time, as we would like to be. We're only human.

When you told me that you were suddenly going on a business trip to Boston, my heart sank. We both know that your friend B lives there. Forgive my fear. Forgive me for wishing that you were less charming, less attractive. I'm convinced that everyone finds you as irresistible as I do. I know what it is to feel the warmth of your smile, and I can't be surprised when others want to bask in that beautiful sunshine.

Even though I'm in love, I've not lost the use of my senses. It's certainly come to my ears that there was something going on between you and B. I wanted so much to trust you, but after last week, I couldn't ignore it anymore. I'm not usually jealous, but, when I saw you with B, I knew that you were more than just old friends. I would have to be blind, or less in love with you, not to notice your long and very private conversation. I felt suddenly shut out — I, who ought to be the closest person in the world to you.

You let B flirt with you, when only *I* am entitled to look at you and laugh with you in that special way. Worse still, instead of being shocked by B's behavior, you actually seemed to enjoy it.

Is there something I should know? Is there something you have been afraid to tell me? (Only to be forgiven and taken back — you needn't be afraid of losing me.)

And even if B is nothing special to you, this raises a larger question. Can I ever deal with your flirtatiousness? You remind me of a rose in the wind — irresponsibly spreading your fragrance and petals for everyone to enjoy. Whereas I want you to be an inviolable rose, blooming solely for me.

I've said a lot of strong things here, maybe too much. I'd like to say even more. But it's time for me to be silent, to give you room to speak. Please answer this letter. I am snatching at excuses for you, and I beg you to prove me wrong in my suspicions.

While I write this, my heart is breaking for love of you, but I couldn't bear to be deceived by the person on whom all my happiness is centered. I feel terrible — when I think of you leaning towards B in that confidential manner, I feel something breaking inside me, too deep for tears. I can't bear to think of B's shadow falling between your lips and mine.

The Defensive Lover
a reassurance

I'm so sorry that you are in pain. That is my first concern because it's the last thing I'd ever want you to feel.

Sweetheart – my only love – you are wrong. You do me wrong. I could never be interested in anyone else but you. What you have heard has no more foundation than what you think you have seen. This is all a terrible misunderstanding.

It was you *yourself* who told me not to wear my heart so obviously on my sleeve and not to talk to you exclusively, and not to wear that lovesick look on my face when I'm around you.

Last night, there was nowhere else I wanted to be except at your side, but I was afraid of monopolizing you as usual, so I talked to an old friend, someone I trust. If you saw an intent look on my face, a soft expression, then it was because I was talking about *you*, and telling B about the great love I've found in you.

Maybe there is a deeper problem – that my fun-loving activities and my friends are proving an obstacle for us, in that you will always want me to be restrained and cool with everyone else except you. You can't ask a rose to lock its perfume up inside its petals. That's not me, and never will be, and you have to understand that. Don't forget what attracted you in the first place.

Please, remember always – my mouth is yours, my arms are yours, my heart is yours – only yours.

When I am with you tomorrow night, I will make you apologize for suspecting me and put an end to this painful nonsense.

P.S. Did you know that I still kiss the phone when I hear it's your voice?

The Penitent Lover

a confession, and a plea for forgiveness

I can't let a minute go past without thinking of you, painful as that is, under the circumstances – circumstances that I've made myself, through my own stupidity.

I'm also writing to you because I want to tell you everything. You deserve complete honesty. I can't hide anything from you any more than I can hide it from my own conscience.

Yes, I was unfaithful, but it was momentary, drunken and ridiculous. Please believe me! How could I have wasted my tremendous love for you on such a person, whose intellect is nowhere near yours, and whose reputation is from hell?

I've put one hundred miles and one hundred years between B and me.

I've been an idiot. I'm ashamed even to beg forgiveness. If you can't forgive me – and why should you really? – can you please grant me one last wish? Could we meet just one more time? I need to see your face, to know what I have lost.

Your face, I will carry in my memory for ever. Even when you've forbidden me, I will still see that face every time I look up; I will still feel the warmth of your smile and remember your lips, with desire, with *ferocious* desire, and all the pleasure they have given me. And I will forever miss my best friend.

But, but – I must ask you, though I hardly dare – won't you forgive and forget?

This is the first time we've ever quarrelled and if you can ever forgive me, I promise it will be the last. Let me make it up to you – or at least let me *try*. I am just dust and ashes until I hear from you.

I know I've betrayed your love and trust, but you alone have the key to my heart. It is as Oliver Wendell Holmes says:

Every person's feelings have a front door and a side-door by which they may be entered. The front-door is on the street. Some keep it always open, some keep it latched, some locked, some bolted ... this front door leads to a passage, which opens into an ante-room, and this into the interior apartments. The side-door opens at once into the secret chambers.

You can keep the world out from your front-door but those of your own flesh and blood, or of certain grades of intimacy can come in at the side-door, if they will, at any hour and in any mood ... and can play the whole gamut of your sensibilities in semi-tones ... Be careful to whom you give a side-door key.

You still have the key. No one else. Please don't lock me out.

·89·

... SHALL I
SEE YOU
AGAIN? THE
IDEA THAT I
SHALL NOT
MAKES ME
SHUDDER.
YOU WILL
TELL ME:
"CONSOLE
YOURSELF."
VERY WELL,
BUT HOW?
FALL IN
LOVE?
IMPOSSIBLE.
FIRST, I
WOULD HAVE
TO FORGET
YOUR
TWITCHES.
GO ABROAD?
STRANGLE
MYSELF? GET
MARRIED? ALL
THESE
THINGS
PRESENT
GREAT
DIFFICULTIES;
I AM LOATH
TO DO ANY OF
THEM ...

Alexander Pushkin
to Anna Petrovna
Kern.

·90·

The Disarming Lover
a truce

We have always told each other the truth. That's why I was so honest when your behavior went over the edge. Even at the risk of losing you, I must still be honest. I can't grovel to you, because really, I haven't done anything to hurt you.

But since we fought, I've just shrivelled up inside. The strange thing is that I feel like a little child who has been beaten for behaving badly, and the one person whom I want to console me is *you* – the very person who handed out the punishment.

If we think about it, a lot of things contributed to the explosion last week. We'd both had bad days, and I think that the balance of bad temper was pretty equal between us. I lost my temper, but it was only because I love you so much. When I thought you'd been unfaithful, I lost control. What *you* saw as a display of anger was in fact just the fireworks of heated jealousy – I couldn't stand the thought that I might lose you. If I thought that this anger in itself might lead to losing you, I'd have fought harder to suppress it.

I still love you more than ever, and I want you to come and lick these wounds you have inflicted. But I'm not going to act like the guilty villain. Let's meet on equal ground and forget all our stupidity and pride. Even though we are sometimes petulant and obsessive, our relationship is worth far more. Let's make a resolution to leave our jobs and our problems *in the office* from now on. There's no perfect love out there waiting. Let's enjoy the one we have, and make it better.

The Forgiving Lover
all's well that ends well

Thank you for your letter. Apart from the pain of separation, what you said hasn't hurt me. It was a small matter and it is already forgotten. There's nothing to forgive.

All that happened is that we both said and did stupid things. There's no reason to turn off the stars, dismantle the moon or put out the sun. Which is what life would be like if you were to be taken away from me.

The best thing about a misunderstanding is the making-up. Come round as soon as you can, and let us make it up to each other with interest. (I've heard the rates are very high these days!)

I love you, oh my flesh and my blood! I die of love, of an endless

The Lunatic Lover
an appeal for Passion, or Nothing

I always knew that love could turn me inside out, but I never understood before that it could turn me into someone else. I've been trying to leave you alone, as I promised. Believe me. I'm trying to respect your need for time, even though it's costing me my sanity. I keep trying to persuade myself that I must leave you in peace, that I've already tormented both of us too much with this crazed and wild passion I have for you. I know that I'm distressing you, and this upsets me even more, because I love you more than I love myself.

When you rejected me, I tried to to let my pride crush my love for you. But love like this doesn't retain any memories of the word "No". "No" disappears, is buried and forgotten. Love like this only looks at the future. Love like this pursues its own fierce, hot desires.

I wasn't made to be sensible. I was made mad and careless. I was made to fall relentlessly in love with someone like you. I want you, who are so precious that the world is too cheap for you. I know I can't have you, and yet I taunt and torture myself with the possibility of having you.

You may do with me whatever you want. The only thing I can't accept is for you to call me your "friend" after all that we've done together. I don't want that gross, thick, homespun commonplace thing called 'friendship'. It's like asking me to a party and then making me sit outside with my nose pressed against the window. I reject it utterly. I sweep it off the bargaining table. Give that to your stupid lovers, the ones with room in their empty hearts for others but you.

Nothing but extremes can help me – either be more cruel so I can maybe learn to hate you, or give in to me and be mine. Your cruelty, of course, will not cure my love. It would take the edge off my hope, but damned despair will gnaw my heart forever.

I don't *care* that my analyst says you are just a narcissistic love-object. You're *my* narcissistic love-object.

I have two luxuries to brood over in my walks, your Loveliness and the hour of my death. O that I could have possession of them both in the same minute. I hate the world: it batters too much the wings of my self-will, and would I could take a sweet poison from your lips to send me out of it.

John Keats to
Fanny Brawne

Alfred
de Musset
to
Georges
Sand

nameless   *love, an insensate, desperate …*   *lost love!*

The Forlorn Lover
an incurable love

> I HAVE ALREADY TOLD YOU THAT THESE WORDS ARE ENGRAVED ON MY HEART, AND THAT THEY PRONOUNCE MY DOOM: TO LOVE YOU, TO SEE YOU, OR TO CEASE TO EXIST.
>
> Julie L'Espinasse to Comte de Guibert

·92·

> IT WOULD BE TOO CRUEL TO SAY TO A WRETCH THAT DIES OF LOVE THAT HE MUST NOT DIE. THE BULLS WOUNDED IN THE CIRCUS HAVE PERMISSION TO GO TO A CORNER AND DIE THERE IN PEACE WITH THE MATADOR'S SWORD IN THEIR SHOULDER.
>
> Alfred de Musset to George Sand

Thank you for turning me down so gently, but I'm in too much pain to stay silent. I'm desolate. You haunt me in my sleep; even more when I'm awake. I feel dead and buried, and yet I'm still desperately alive — alive, but, without you, without a life.

I haven't had one minute's peace since I saw you, for in that same moment I loved you and also realized that you were committed to someone else. Other arms have held you, and you have changed partners before. Why couldn't you change to me? Every time you are with someone else, I feel you are trespassing on my happiness — betraying me.

I swore that I would fight this love, and somehow disentangle my heart from yours. I have fought it with wine, with parties, even with constant exposure to you, in the hope that your indifference would finally kill my unreciprocated feelings. But at the end of each day, I return at night to my unhappy self, having to account truthfully to my heart for the pain I have caused it. Thoughts of you rise up inside me, take my hand, lead me to my lonely bed, and leave me there to cry for you. And that is the best of it, to cry for you — probably the closest I'll ever get to you.

The day is as beautiful as you and the night has too much of your scent. Your last fond kiss burns on my cheek. Why not my lips? Your understanding smile is far too small a sliver of the moon.

None of the wildest endearments I have sent you are in any way withdrawn. I am incurable. The world would have less tragedy in it, if I hadn't met you, but would it be a world worth living in? Your name is etched in my heart forever. I dare not let you go.

(Inspired by letters from Thomas Otway and Luigi Pirandello.)

✱ ✱ INCONSOLABLE ✱ ✱

(Edith Wharton thought of sending a cable like this to
W. Morton Fullerton, in June 1908.)

The Semi-Detached Lover

a morning-after letter

Let me write these few lines, which are bedewed with my scalding tears … in the hours of my passionate sorrow peopled with terrible phantasmagoria, disgust seiozes me of the entire world, a general distrust tortures me, and in a gloomy, gloomy state of mind I shall totter towards the grave …

Ugo Foscolo to Isabella Roncioni

You don't deserve this letter, but I'm trying with my whole heart to explain something painful and delicate.

Last night I told you that I loved you. I won't deny it, and you don't need to remind me. But I need you to understand that what I said isn't exactly true. I meant it when I said it, but having spent the last day without you, I realize that it is not true. What I felt was *excitement*, not love.

There's a world of difference between exhilarating infatuation, which engulfs me every time I see you, and real love, which takes time to build, which survives separations and burrows deeply into the heart. You see, when we're apart, my feelings for you return to mere fondness. The passion never lasts longer than our meeting, and I think that this is the key to the way things are between us. This is not a romance, even though the sensations are pleasant.

You are a beautiful person. You can always make me laugh. I *approve* of you entirely. You're the kind of person I want as a life-long friend, a dear friend, maybe my dearest friend. I want to smother your sweet body with kisses, but it is not *love* that I feel then. It is *desire*.

I'm weak. I can't promise to be strong. You'll cast your usual spells over me when I see you next, and I may well say those fatal words again. If you want me to be sensible, then you must develop a talent for being boring and ugly. I guess that's not going to happen.

I'll understand if you refuse to see me again, because that's probably all I deserve, but I hope you will not. (We *are* good together, after all …)

The Relinquishing Lover

It's been great.

If only you had...

·94·

IT WAS *just* ONE OF *those* THINGS.

I just wish...

I'M *no good* FOR YOU.

My conscience will no longer let me keep you all to myself.

Just a few weeks ago, I could never have dreamed that I would write a letter like this to you. I aimed every love letter like a paper dart at your heart. Every morning, I ran to the mailbox, like a thirsty dog to water, hoping for your reply.

I've loved all the time we've spent together, I've been enriched by it, and I will always remember it with pleasure. Yes – *remember*. I'm so sorry, but it's over.

I think we've been fooling ourselves. Maybe the love we had was more of an infatuation – the kind that's too hot to burn for long. I know now that it's not the kind that can last, nor does it have anything truly substantial to it. I will always love you, but I've stopped being *in love* with you, and it is time to stop acting like your lover.

I know that I must end this now, before we end up trapped in a marriage that would be a mistake. I know that you couldn't go on much longer loving me without any commitment on my part. It's heartbreaking watching you try to please me more, in all kinds of thoughtful little ways, as if being 'good' would help you win me as a kind of prize. It's so painful to keep having these arguments about our relationship, with me always finally giving in to keep you from doing something desperate. You'll never be satisfied with me, and I agree you deserve more.

I know that my withdrawal of affection will do you a great wrong and a great hurt, but how can you still want me to love you? Think about it. How can you want someone who does not want you *completely*? How can someone of your sensitivity be content with nothing but kindness in exchange for your tenderness, and nothing but affectionate respect in return for the extraordinary, but undeserved, passion you lavish on me?

I kiss you tenderly, but firmly, goodbye.

NEVER SAY, "I HAVE LOST THIS," BUT SAY, "I HAVE GIVEN IT BACK."
Epictetus

The Abandoned Lover

I was devastated by your letter. When I read it, I thought I had woken up in someone else's life.

Are you serious? Have I really known you at all, all this time? Have I been a momentary luxury? An experiment? Is that all? How can you sum me up and dismiss me in a single, shocking letter. Were all your love letters lies?

The trouble is that even if I could convince myself emotionally that you are no longer responding, there are still so many rational reasons to love you. You are so fascinating, so charismatic, so creative and so thoughtful. How dare you come into my life, and make me unzip myself like a coat and zip you up inside? You, were supposed to be there forever.

And the worst thing is that I can't understand. You won't see me, and you won't talk to me, so how can I ask what I did wrong, in order to beg your forgiveness. You probably won't even read this letter.

I got your letter. I understand.

But, Oh ...

Without me, who is going to walk with you in the rain?

Without me, who is going to hold you all night?

Without me, who is going to listen to your stories?

Without me, who is going to touch your body till it cries?

What could I possibly have done? How can I have hurt you? Why would I hurt the person I love most in the world? That would only be another way of hurting myself.

Tell me it's not true. Everything is sinister, terrible, alien – even this apartment where we've been so happy together, the street corner we've always passed hand-in-hand. Your clothes are still here, your toothbrush too. I spent the night in the bed we've shared with such pleasure. I met your ghost there, calling my name, and the ghost of our life together, full of tears and caresses, full of you. I am writing this now in that bedroom, where too much has happened for me to be able to bear.

I will never stop kissing you. I won't appeal to your pity, I can only appeal to love – my love for you, and your love for me. It is real, it has nourished us both for many years. You're not just a watercolour that washes off. The stain of you won't come out of my life, not ever.

The Inextinguishable Lover
a gracious retreat

This will be a most welcome letter from me, because it's the last one. I wouldn't have tried so hard if ... had not encouraged me. But I see now that it's hopeless. I'll stop harrassing you, and I offer nothing now except my good wishes for your future happiness.

I hope that when you do fall in love, it's with someone who loves you as much as I love you – passionately, with commitment and utter honesty. Meanwhile, these words from Trumbull Stickney say what I felt as I burned all your love letters last night, feeding them one after another into the fire.

I give you back your heart, with permission to do whatever you like with it.

> ... DESIRE
> REVIVES LIKE FERNS ON A NOVEMBER FIRE.
>
> IT COMES TO ONLY A MEMORY.
> WE HAVE TOO MANY MEMORIES,
> AND SOMEHOW I BELIEVE WE DIE
> OF THINGS LIKE THESE,
> LOVING WHAT WAS NOT, MIGHT NOT BE,
> NOR IS ...
>
> LIKE A PEARL DROPPED IN RED DARK WINE,
> YOUR PALE FACE SANK WITHIN MY HEART,
> NOT TO BE MINE, YET ALWAYS MINE.

The cruel agonies, the poignant struggles, the bitter tears have been replaced by a tender companion, pale and gentle Melancholy. This morning, after a tranquil night, I found her at my bedside, with a sweet smile on her lips. This is the friend that will go with me. She bears your last kiss on her forehead.

Alfred de Musset to George Sand

Acknowledgements
Textual

Every effort has been made to locate all copyright-holders. In the event that we have unwillingly or inadvertently omitted the proper notification, the editor would be grateful to hear from the copyright-holder, and undertakes to amend following editions accordingly.

The publishers gratefully acknowledge the permission of the following to reproduce copyrighted material in this book:

"somewhere i have never travelled,gladly beyond" is reprinted from COMPLETE POEMS, 1904–62 by E. E. Cummings, edited by George J. Firmage, by permission of W.W. Norton & Company Ltd. Copyright © 1979, 1991 by the Trustees for the E. E. Cummings Trust and George J. Firmage.

"Kisses" from Call Yourself Alive? The Poetry of Nina Cassian, translated from the Romanian by Andrea Deletant and Brenda Walker, published by Forest Books in 1988, reprinted in 1989 and 1992. Copyright © 1988 Nina Cassian, Translations Copyright © 1988 Andrea Deletant and Brenda Walker

"In There" from Poems 1963–1983 by C.K. Williams, published by Bloodaxe Books in the UK and Farrar Straus & Giroux, Inc in the USA in 1988. Copyright © 1969, 1988 by C.K. Williams.

"The innocence of any flesh sleeping" from Love Poems by Brian Patten, published by Flamingo, an imprint of HarperCollins Publishers, in 1992. Copyright © Brian Patten 1981, 1984.

Extract from "The Gardener" from Collected Poems and Plays of Rabindranath Tagore. Copyright © 1913 Macmillan Publishing Company, renewed 1941 by Rabindranath Tagore. Reprinted by permission of Simon & Schuster, Inc.

"You who never arrived" from Collected Poetry of Rainer Maria Rilke, translated by Stephen Mitchell. Published by Picador in the UK in 1987, Random House, Inc. in the USA, with the cooperation of Insel Verlag, Germany. Translations copyright © Stephen Mitchell 1980, 1981, 1982.

"The First Marriage" by Peter Meinke. Copyright © Peter Meinke 1991, reprinted by permission of the author.

"Just Loving You" by Stephanie June Sorréll reproduced by permission of the author. Copyright © Stephanie June Sorréll 1995

Extract from letter from Olive Lewis to Leslie Couzens reproduced courtesy of Mrs Ann Judge and the Imperial War Museum, London.

Old Love-Letter-Writing Manuals referred to in the text, but not described in the historical section (please note that the following are not necessarily first editions, but are the material extant in the British Library):
The New Academy of Complements, 1671;
Wit's Improvement Or, A New Academy of Complements, 1715;
How to Write – A Pocket Manual, 1804;
The Art of Writing, John Newbery (second edition, 1748);
A Compleat INTRODUCTION to the ART of WRITING LETTERS by S. Johnson, 1758;
The Complete Letter Writer, or Polite English Secretary (fifth edition 1758, sixteenth edition in 1778);
THE ART OF CORRESPONDENCE, ENGLISH AND FRENCH, by Percy Sadler (sixth edition by 1870).

Illustrative

Collage on the endpapers by Mandy Pritty, including Victorian Scraps, care of Mamelok Press, Bury St Edmunds, England. Letter from John Keats to Fanny Brawne on front cover reproduced by permission of The London Borough of Camden from the Collections at Keats House, Hampstead, London, England. Calligraphy on first and last pages by Alan Peacock.

Personal

With very special thanks to the following (in alphabetical order)
for contributing their real love, suffering and professional expertise to the manuscript:
Dr Bruce Barker-Benfield, Kristina Blagojevitch, Abraham Borenstein, Brian Burns, Yvonne Dawe, David Franks, Phillip Herriot, Jenny and Melissa Lovric, Fred and Wendy Oliver, Melissa Stein, Andreas Thenhaus, Martin Thornton, Suzanne Wolstenholme

We lay aside letters never to read them again, and in the end we destroy them for reasons of discretion, and there disappears the most beautiful, the most immediate breath of life, irrecoverably for ourselves and for others.

Johann Wolfgang
von Goethe